THE **STORY** OF
DIKRAN

THE **STORY** OF
DIKRAN

*The impossible true story of a
little Armenian Gampr*

DAVID M. GUILD

ELITE

Xulon Press Elite
2301 Lucien Way #415
Maitland, FL 32751
407.339.4217
www.xulonpress.com

Printed in the United States of America.

ISBN-13: 9781545618523

Acknowledgements

WHILE DIKRAN HAS TOUCHED MANY PEOPLE along his journey, there are those who have touched Dikran's life and made this amazing dog's journey possible in the first place. There are also those who helped me in different ways as I set out to write this book. Without these people, this book would not have happened, and I owe each of them a huge debt of gratitude.

Ovsanna Hovsepyan and her dog rescue group Dingo Team in Yerevan, Armenia:
Thank you for rescuing Dikran and seeing value in the life of a starved and disfigured little runt. And thank you for having the vision to look as far and wide as you did to find Laura and her group in Southern California, all for the little dog with the crooked legs.

Coastal German Shepherd Rescue in Southern California:
Thank you for putting Dikran under your umbrella and helping to find him a home. Dikran is no German shepherd, but you were still there for him.

Laura Manukian:
Thank you to Dikran's "Auntie Laura" in Southern California for your stubborn persistence in getting

Dikran to America and finding the right home for a unique dog and his "special needs." You got him to our facility, and then you told me that I needed to adopt him, that he needed me, and I needed him. You were right, and I will always think of you as the person who gave me this most amazing dog.

Brian, Cathy, Claire, Jerry, Sophia, and Tom:
Thank you to the models that I used for the sketches in this book. I had already written the manuscript when I began my search for the right people to represent each character. I already had a picture in my head of each character, and God led me to you. If I were an expert artist, I could not have drawn a better representation of Ben, Rebecca, Grandma and Grandpa, Mom, and Greg than what I saw in each of you.

My son, John, and my wife, Paula:
Thank you, John, for being Dikran's best friend right from the beginning. The two of you have a special bond that made it easy for Dikran to love joining our family. Thank you, Paula, for all of the love and support you gave Dikran, from caring for his physical needs the moment he showed up at our facility, to the help and understanding it took to bring him into our family, and for the support I needed as I wrote this story.

Prologue

BEN SAT IN THE CHAIR OUTSIDE OF THE SCHOOL counselor's office and thought about what had just happened. He didn't think it was fair that he was in trouble. *All I did was try to save a dog,* he thought to himself.

As he sat there, Mr. Tanner, the school counselor, opened the door and invited him into the office. Mr. Tanner was a large, burly man, and every boy in the school was a little bit afraid of him. The only thing that made Ben feel better was that this was the end of the last day of school. Fifth grade was finally going to be behind him.

"Come on in, Benjamin." Mr. Tanner gestured to a chair that was right in front of his desk. "Have a seat."

Ben sat in the chair, noticing that his short legs didn't even reach close to the floor. This made him feel a little uncomfortable. Looking up, he saw that Mr. Tanner was now sitting in his own seat, staring intently across the desk right into his eyes. This made him feel even more uncomfortable.

Mr. Tanner spoke, slowly and with a deep voice. "Benjamin, I know this is the last day of school and that you are excited about going to visit your grandparents. But you ignored a teacher, and you started a fight with another student. A student, I might add, who is twice as big as you." He paused for a moment while Ben looked down at his dirty and torn shirt and the scrapes on his knees. As he looked down, bits of dirt fell out of his thick, black hair. "What do you have to say for yourself?"

"Honest, Mr. Tanner. I was only trying to stop that little dog from running into the street. I was afraid he would get hit by a car."

"And Mrs. McAllistair was afraid *you* were going to run out into the street and get hit by a car. She said that you almost did get hit. You can't take it into your own hands to save every dog you see. And then you started a fight with Steven Keller, the biggest boy in the fifth grade. Why did you do that?"

"He called that poor dog a runt. Then he…" Ben hesitated, then looked down at his folded hands. He just silently sat there.

"Benjamin," Mr. Tanner prompted. "What were you about to say? I want you to be completely honest with me."

Ben hesitated again before speaking in a very quiet voice. "He called me a runt too."

Mr. Tanner frowned. "It was wrong of him to say that. Did he say anything else?"

Ben sat quietly for a moment, looking at the floor. "That was all."

The look on Mr. Tanner's face indicated that he knew that there was more, but he didn't push Ben. "Benjamin, I know that it has been hard at home since your father… left. Your mom works long hours trying to make ends meet, and your older sister does so much to help. Think about that this summer. Look to your sister for help. She tutors other kids here at school, and I'm sure she could help you more with your studies. Acting out like this won't help your grades or make things any easier on your mom. You are a good kid, Ben. You have a lot to offer, okay? Just think about it."

Ben looked a little relieved. "Okay, Mr. Tanner. Thank you. Is… is that all?"

"Yes, that is all. And, Benjamin?"

"Yes, Mr. Tanner?"

"Have a good and safe summer. See you next year."

"Thanks, Mr. Tanner."

As Ben left the office and started to walk home, he looked up and saw Steven Keller heading his way. *Oh, brother,* Ben thought. *Just what I need now.*

Steven started walking with Ben, and he had a big smile on his face. But when he spoke, Ben knew that the smile wasn't real. "Hey, runt. Mr. Tanner going to make you sit in the corner all summer?"

"No, Steven. Just leave me alone."

"Okay, runt. Go have fun chasing those dumb stray dogs around. And I'll be seeing you next year."

The "dumb dog" comment made Ben angry. "They aren't dumb. They just don't have a family."

"Right." Steven was walking away, but he stopped and turned around. "Those dogs you are always trying to save are just like you, runt. They don't have a family because nobody wants them, just like you had to be adopted because nobody wanted you. That's also why your new father left. You aren't really his, and he didn't want you." Steven laughed and walked away.

Ben was red in the face, and he went back and forth between angry and sad. His new father had left without warning several years ago, just a month after he had been adopted, and he still struggled with feelings of abandonment. He couldn't help but think that it was his fault.

As he walked, deep in his thoughts, his sister Rebecca came skipping up next to him. Her long brown ponytail swished back and forth as she skipped along, and she was in a happy mood. "Hi, Ben. I heard you picked another fight with Steven Keller." She looked at his unruly appearance. "Looks like you lost again."

"Hi, Becca." Ben looked up at her happy face. "I was just—"

"—I know." Rebecca knew her brother well. "You were trying to save that little dog. Mom won't be happy. She just bought that shirt."

Ben nodded his head. "But at least it is summer! I can't wait until we leave for Grandma and Grandpa's farm. We leave Sunday morning, right?"

"Yup. Right after church." Rebecca had a big smile on her face. She loved church *and* going to her grandparent's farm.

"Ugh!" Ben did not share her enthusiasm. "Why can't we skip church and leave earlier?"

"Ben! We need to thank God for all that we have. Can't you see that?"

Ben shook his head and looked at his bumps, bruises, and torn shirt. "All I see is that I'm going to be in trouble as soon as Mom gets home. I don't think that God really cares about me at all, if there even is a God."

Rebecca shook her head but said nothing. She knew from past talks with her brother where this conversation was going. Ben would say that he was the smallest kid in his class, he got picked on all of the time, he didn't have any friends, and that his father had left him. She knew that he still sometimes felt like he didn't belong. After all, he had been adopted, and Rebecca was her mom's *real* daughter. How could a kind and loving God let all of that happen? So Benjamin and Rebecca finished the short walk home in silence, each lost in their own thoughts.

Chapter 1

"**H**URRY UP, BEN! WE DON'T WANT TO BE LATE for church!" Ben's mom always had to hurry him up for church. He never liked going, but it wasn't so bad today. Soon they would be on their way to the farm, and that put Ben in a good mood. Besides, he hadn't really gotten in too much trouble for messing up his new shirt. Maybe Mom was in a good mood too. All Ben knew was that they would be headed for the country in a short time.

As they pulled into the church parking lot, Ben's mom turned around and looked at him. "Ben, please try to pay attention during Sunday school. We're all packed and will be leaving for the farm as soon as we get home. We will be on the road before you know it, okay?"

"Okay," Ben groaned. "I'll try. I just don't like listening to stuff I don't believe in."

Ben's mom sighed to herself and took his answer to mean that he would try to behave.

Two hours later they were pulling out of their driveway and heading north toward the open country. The yearly trip to the farm was the best part of the summer, and Ben could hardly contain himself.

Rebecca was just as excited, and his mom seemed to be as excited as they were.

Ben knew that his mom had grown up on the farm and had lived there until she graduated from high school and got married. He wasn't sure why she had moved to the city, but Rebecca had told him it had something to do with needing to make more money. Rebecca said that her father didn't always work, and that Mom needed to help by getting a job.

Ben looked out of the car window and thought that his mom probably missed her family. Maybe that was why they always went back to the farm each year as soon as school got out. Ben shrugged his shoulders as his mind went to the farm. He couldn't wait to get there. Grandma's fresh farm cooking, swimming in the creek, helping Grandpa fix things around the farm, and seeing all the new farm animals was something Ben and Rebecca looked forward to each year.

But the most wonderful part of all was at the end of each day after supper and dessert: storytime with Grandpa. Down by the creek with a mug of Grandma's special hot cocoa, with a blanket to keep warm from the cool early summer evening breeze, Rebecca and Ben would curl up and listen to Grandpa as he would tell a story.

Sometimes the story would be about an exciting hero from the past and sometimes, about some mythical, faraway place. Whatever the story was about, they loved the way Grandpa would tell the tale. He was so good at it, and they would wait all day long for the next story, for they would get a new one each evening. Ben was daydreaming about one of the stories from last summer when his mom brought him back to reality.

"Ben, what was the lesson about in church this morning? Do you remember?"

Ben thought for a moment. "Something about Jesus being a shepherd and us being sheep, I think. Some weird thing like that."

"That sounds like a good lesson. We are like a bunch of lost sheep."

"It sounds weird to me. I'm not a sheep, and I don't need a shepherd."

Rebecca spoke up. "I think we had the same lesson in my class. We *are* like lost sheep, Ben. That is why we need Jesus. He shows us the way."

Ben made a funny face. "Maybe you are a sheep. I'm not, and I don't need Jesus to show me any way, either."

Ben's mom was very patient. "That's okay, Ben. Maybe a bit later in life you will understand. Just know that Jesus loves you. Your sister and I love you too."

This was getting too mushy for Ben, so he just leaned back in his seat and pretended to go to sleep. He pictured himself already at the farm, having fun doing all of the things he was looking forward to. Ben actually was kind of tired. He hadn't slept much the night before, and though he was excited about going to the farm, he slowly drifted off into sleep.

"Ben!" Rebecca's voice cut through his sleep. "Ben, wake up! We're here!"

Ben jolted out of his sleep so fast he bumped his head on the front seat of the car. "We are here already?

How… what… YAY!!" Ben couldn't believe it. They were already there, and Grandma and Grandpa were coming down the steps from the front porch to greet them.

Ben was out of the car as soon as it stopped moving, running to greet his grandparents. Rebecca was right there with him. "Grandpa Roger! Grandma Alice!" Hugs were exchanged as the kids literally ran into their grandparents' open arms.

Grandma and Grandpa looked up as their daughter got out of the car. Grandpa was the first to speak. "Hello, Brenda. I see you brought two little firecrackers up here to visit." He smiled at the two kids, and they smiled right back. "Let me help the two of you unload the car. I think your grandmother just might have a little something ready for supper. If, that is, there are any hungry people around here."

He looked around to see if he could find anyone who was hungry.

"We are starved!" Rebecca and Ben shouted at the same time. They had forgotten that the car ride had taken all afternoon. "What's for supper?"

"Easy, easy." Grandpa had a big smile on his face. "Remember the rules. First, we unload the car and move you into your rooms; *then* we can eat. Deal?"

"Deal!" The two kids turned and raced back to the car, Grandpa strolling behind them to help. Their mom and Grandma were headed to the house.

Ben looked at the farmhouse as he hauled the last load of stuff out of the car. It was just as he had remembered: a big two-story house that looked... well, it looked just like a farmhouse *should* look. There was even smoke coming out of the chimney, and the smell of the fire in the fireplace had to compete with the smell of Grandma's fried chicken. And behind the house was the big red barn with lots of farm animals. There were big pastures on either side of the house, and in the quiet of the evening Ben could just hear the creek that ran along the backside of the farmland.

Ben was happy. Here everything was right. He really loved the farm, and he wished he could stay forever, with nothing to worry about and no one to pick on him. As he climbed the stairs to his bedroom, his mind wandered back to his earliest memories. He remembered being in a foster family in the city and how he had never gotten along with any of the other children in that family. Then there were one or two other foster families. It was so different from the peaceful life he experienced every summer here on the farm. His new family was different. His mom and sister really seemed to love him, and his grandparents were the best.

He dropped the last load on his bed and looked out of his bedroom window. His bedroom was in the back of the second story of the house, and the window looked out to the barn and the creek beyond. He smiled to himself. *This place could almost make me believe in God.* He looked out the window for a few more seconds, and then turned to head down to supper. "Almost," he repeated out loud.

Chapter 2

SUPPER WAS DELICIOUS. THERE WAS FRIED chicken, mashed potatoes and gravy, corn on the cob, cold fresh milk, and hot apple pie that was right out of the oven. Ben's mom was a good cook, but she worked long hours, so she usually picked up something on her way home. Neither of the kids complained, but they absolutely *loved* Grandma's home cooking. Despite his small size, Ben cleaned his plate and gladly had seconds. Rebecca didn't have quite the appetite that Ben had, but she finished all of the food on her plate too.

Ben stayed out of the supper conversation. The adults talked mostly about how things were going for Ben's mom at work, how she was working such long hours, and how she didn't want to take any money from Grandma and Grandpa.

Ben knew that, when the adults talked about adult things, he was not supposed to interrupt, and Rebecca knew it too. That was okay because both of them, as much as they loved the food, wanted to hurry up and finish. They knew that Grandpa had gotten a new horse, and they couldn't wait to go see him. But what they really wanted was to head down to the creek for storytime, and it was already getting dark.

Ben waited for a break in the conversation. "Mom, is it okay if Becca and I clear our places and go check out the barn?"

Ben's mom knew what he wanted, so she looked to her father. "Dad?"

Grandpa leaned back in his chair and smiled. "It's okay. But stay out of the stall. Raider is still new here, and he doesn't know you yet. You may look at him, but no touching." Grandpa knew that Rebecca would keep her brother in line. "And one more thing."

"Yes, Grandpa?"

"Don't be too long. I think we have an appointment down at the creek, unless you are all too tired and want to go straight to bed." Grandpa sure liked to tease them.

"No way!" Ben was clearing his place as fast as he could, Rebecca not far behind.

"Children! Children, slow down. Let's not break anything." Their mom tried to sound serious, but she was having a hard time not laughing.

After clearing his place, Ben turned to Grandpa before heading out to the barn. "Grandpa, what's the story about tonight? Please just give me a hint. *Please?*" Ben knew that Grandpa liked to surprise them with his stories and not tell them anything in advance.

"Hmm." Grandpa leaned back in his chair and put his hand to his chin as though he was in deep thought. "Tonight the story is about a dog. It is a true story about a very special dog, and that is all I am telling you. Now run along before it gets to be too late."

"Yippee!" Ben was so excited he could barely see straight as he ran to the barn. "A dog story! A true dog story!"

The barn was huge and very dark, but Rebecca remembered where the light switch was. She turned it on, and the barn was flooded with light. There was a large open area at the front, then a lot of pens and stalls for a variety of different animals. Right in the middle of the open area was the big farm tractor that Ben had always wanted to drive. "When you are old enough," Grandpa would tell him every year. The two kids walked around the tractor and headed to the back of the stalls where the new horse was, making sure not to speak too loudly or make too much noise with their feet.

At the back of the barn, in the biggest stall, was a huge Persian horse. It was the biggest horse either of them had ever seen.

"Wow!" Ben was so impressed with the size of the horse that he almost forgot about the upcoming story.

"Well," Rebecca spoke quietly, "last year Grandpa said that he needed a horse that could pull his farm carts in case the tractor ever broke down."

"It sure looks like Raider could pull just about any-thing." Ben smiled. "I'd sure like to see him pull old Steven Keller around for a while."

"Ben!" Rebecca's voice was stern, but she was trying not to laugh.

They spent another minute or two looking at Raider. Then they looked at each other, nodded, and headed back to the house. Storytime with, they hoped, Grandma's hot cocoa.

When they got back to the house, the kitchen work was almost done, and they were happy to notice two mugs on the counter and a pot on the stove with the smell of hot cocoa filling the kitchen. Grandpa came walking into the room with two blankets in his arms and a lantern in his hand. "Are you two ready? The bench and chair are already down by the water." Grandpa seemed as excited as Ben and Rebecca, and the two were so excited they could barely carry their cocoa down to the creek without spilling.

The special story place was a cozy clearing, right by the creek, under the branches of two large oak trees. Grandpa had told them a few years ago that he chose this place for the stories because there was a special oak tree there for each of them. It was a great place to settle in and relax after a long day and listen to Grandpa's story. The two children sat on the bench, and Grandpa wrapped a blanket around each of them to keep them warm from the cool breeze. He adjusted his chair so he could sit facing them.

Slowly, Grandpa began. "First things first. This is a different story. It is unlike any story I have ever told you."

"How is it different, Grandpa?" Ben was already on the edge of the bench.

"Well, I usually tell you a new story each night. This story will take the whole week to tell." He paused and looked right at Ben. "That means at the end of each night you will have to wait all the way until the next night for the story to continue, with no questions during the day. Will you be able to do that? That is the rule for this story."

Rebecca was already nodding her head up and down. She was great at following rules. Ben looked a bit shocked. "I have to wait the whole week to hear how it ends? What kind of story takes a week to tell?"

Grandpa chuckled and patted Ben on the shoulder. "How it ends? Ben, this story is still happening. But there is much to tell, and I think you will love every bit of it. In fact, I will guarantee you that this will be your favorite story of all time. Do we have a deal?"

Ben was so curious and interested that there was no way he wanted to miss out. He stuck out his right hand to shake Grandpa's hand. "Deal."

All three settled in and got comfortable. Grandpa cleared his throat. "Like I said, this is a true story about a very special dog. A breed of dog I am sure you have never heard of in your whole lives."

"Ben knows about every breed of dog." Rebecca knew that her brother studied dogs more than he studied his homework.

"Well," Grandpa responded, "this breed comes from a country on the other side of the world. From a country called Armenia. Do either of you know of any dog breeds from Armenia?"

Ben thought hard for a moment but couldn't think of a single breed. Rebecca couldn't either. "No."

"I didn't think so. I couldn't either, at least not until I heard about this dog."

Ben was already getting into the story. "Was the dog in our story actually born in... how do you say it, Grandpa?"

Grandpa chuckled. "Armenia, Ben. Armenia. It is a bit hard to pronounce until you get the hang of it. And, yes, he was born in Armenia."

Rebecca was also getting into the story. "What is the breed called?"

"He is an Armenian Gampr."

Ben couldn't help but laugh. "A what? Come on, Grandpa. Is this for real? That is the weirdest name for a dog breed."

"It is a real breed, Ben. Not all breeds use English words. The Armenian word 'Gampr' means protector or watchdog. The Armenian farmers use Gamprs to protect their farm animals, like sheep." Grandpa reached into the pocket of his blue jeans and pulled out a picture. He held it in front of Ben and Rebecca and held his lantern close so they could clearly see.

"Wow!" They both leaned forward and saw their first Gampr. Ben looked at Grandpa. "He looks huge."

"He is. And see how he is looking around? He is busy protecting all those sheep."

"Protecting the sheep?" Ben was curious. "Protecting them from what?"

"Whatever might threaten them. Usually wolves."

It was Rebecca's turn. "You mean Gamprs fight wolves? Don't the wolves kill them?"

"No. Usually it's the other way around. Gamprs are pretty serious dogs. They are huge, ferocious, and they have very heavy coats to protect them. It gets pretty cold in the winter."

"Wow!" Ben liked the story before it had really even started. "Don't they get hurt when they get in fights? I've seen pictures on the Internet of dogs that have been in really bad fights. They are all bit up, especially around the ears."

"That's true," Grandpa agreed. "But the Armenian shepherds learned that lesson thousands of years ago. When the Gamprs are little puppies, they cut their ears off. All the way off."

Ben winced and grabbed his own ears. "Ouch! How gross! And mean! That must really hurt."

"It's not really mean, Ben. They don't want the wolves to have a target to grab. It's much better for the Gamprs to have no ears."

"Does the Gampr in our story have ears?" Rebecca was still holding her own ears.

"He has no ears. It does make them look a little different." Grandpa paused for a moment while Ben and Rebecca finished feeling their own ears, then he continued. "Gamprs have been protecting the farm animals for a long time. They are called guardians, and the name fits. Many scholars believe that King David from the Bible had guardians watching his sheep back when he was a shepherd. That was a long time ago."

Ben made a face at the mention of the Bible. Grandpa saw him but said nothing. He knew that Ben was going to love this story, and he would let that love of story address what Ben believed. He continued with the tale. "Gamprs are working dogs. They spend their whole lives being guardians. Usually it is sheep, but they will guard anything they are told to protect."

Rebecca giggled. "Will they protect chickens or pigs?"

"Chickens or pigs. Or goats and cows. They will guard anything they are told to protect."

Ben perked up. "What about children?"

"They will protect children. Whatever a Gampr is protecting, you don't want to touch. For real, Ben."

"Wow!" Ben thought that was really cool. "Is the Gampr in our story a fierce protector? I'll bet he is the fiercest of all! Meaner than Steven Keller!"

"Well, I will tell you that our Gampr is about the most special one of all. And he has the most incredible story. He is very well known in Armenia, and now he is well known in America, too."

"Does that mean he is here in America now?"

"Yes, he is now in America."

"Really? Where?"

"That is part of the story."

Rebecca spoke before Ben could continue. "Grandpa, what is his name?"

14

"His name, my dear, is Dikran. He is named after a great king from Armenia's past. But for the first part of his life he didn't have a name. In fact, he didn't have anything. Not anything at all."

"Why not?" Both were totally hooked by this time. "How can a dog not have anything? Especially a name?"

"That, my two little bumblebees, is why we are here. This is the story of Dikran."

Chapter 3

BEN AND REBECCA WIGGLED IN THEIR SEATS to get more comfortable. They also adjusted their blankets. They knew that now the story would begin for real, and they were already fascinated. They couldn't wait to hear about Dikran.

Grandpa knew that he had their undivided attention, and he, too, made himself a little more comfortable. The look on his face showed that he was going to enjoy telling the story as much as Ben and Rebecca would enjoy hearing it.

"It was right around the end of November in 2012 when Dikran was born. And just like the other Gampr puppies in his litter, he had his ears cut off."

Ben and Rebecca both reached up and grabbed their ears again but didn't say a word. They wanted Grandpa to continue. But first, Grandpa reached into his pocket and pulled out a picture.

Ben's eyes opened wide. "A picture? Of Dikran?"

Grandpa shook his head. "Not Dikran. This is what Gampr puppies normally look like."

Ben and Rebecca leaned forward on the bench as Grandpa held the picture in front of them. He held up his lantern so they could clearly see the picture.

Rebecca smiled a big smile. "What a cute puppy. He is so adorable."

Ben agreed. "He also looks very healthy."

"Yes he does." Grandpa then continued with the story. "As the puppies grew, their owners noticed four things that weren't right with one of the boy puppies. He wasn't growing like the other puppies, he did not have the thick, heavy coat like the other puppies, and he was very skinny."

As Grandpa paused for a moment, Ben spoke up. "I'll bet he was skinny because the bigger puppies wouldn't let him eat. Grandpa, you said there were four things wrong with him."

"I did, Ben. The fourth problem was that his front legs were becoming deformed. They were twisted and bent in the wrong direction down by his feet. It was affecting his ability to walk. When he would stand, he was so low in the front that he was almost walking on his elbows."

Rebecca looked horrified. "That is so sad. Why were his legs like that?"

"Nobody really knows."

Ben could feel the painful scrapes on his own legs. "Did it hurt little Dikran when he walked on those bent legs?"

"I don't know that either. What I do know is that at some point in time Dikran found himself without a home. It seems like his owners didn't want him because they felt that he was no good to them."

Ben and Rebecca looked at each other in surprise. Ben said, "Did he run away, or did they just toss him out?"

"He probably didn't run away." Grandpa seemed pretty sure of this. "Gamprs love their families and wouldn't just run away. I think that his owners dumped him out somewhere far enough from their farm where he wouldn't find his way back home."

"That is the meanest thing I have ever heard of." Rebecca looked angry, and her face was red. "He couldn't help the way he was. It wasn't his fault that he was small and had crooked legs. How was he going to survive? Didn't anybody love him?"

Ben was silent and looked very thoughtful. Grandpa saw this and knew that Dikran's story was already touching Ben in some very personal ways. He continued. "I don't know how he survived, but he did. Somehow he was able to find enough to eat, at least enough to stay alive. He also managed to find a way to avoid any of the wild dogs or wolves that might have gone after him. But as time went on, he became very, very skinny. There is not much to eat out in the wild during winter."

Ben broke his silence and spoke up. "Wasn't he cold? You said that he didn't have the heavy coat that Gamprs are supposed to have."

"I'm sure that he was *very* cold. And he was starving and not able to walk very well. He was a runt, but I think that he was one tough little boy. He didn't have any companionship either. He was all alone. Maybe he shouldn't have survived, but he did."

Ben was silent again. The word "runt" stirred up a lot of feelings inside of him. So did the feeling of being abandoned and alone. He had only known about Dikran for a few minutes, but he already felt a strong connection to him. He already *loved* this little dog.

Rebecca could not stay silent. She had too many questions. "What happened next, Grandpa? How did he stay alive?"

"Well, somehow he stayed alive, and he eventually wandered into the capital city of Armenia, the city of Yerevan."

Ben repeated the name silently, and then he said it out loud. "Yerevan. Never heard of it. How did Dikran find Yerevan?"

"Yerevan is in the middle of what is called the Armenian Highlands. Dikran was probably born on a farm on the outskirts of Yerevan, and after he was discarded he wandered all over the place looking for food. He just ended up in Yerevan. Look, here is a picture." Grandpa reached again into his pocket and grabbed the lantern.

As he held the picture for Ben and Rebecca to see, they both got wide eyes as they saw the mountains in the background and all of the snow on the rooftops.

Rebecca shivered as she thought of Dikran trying to survive in the cold winter weather. "Was it snowy like this when Dikran was out there?"

Grandpa shrugged. "I don't know. It was winter, so I am sure it was quite cold. But he found his way into Yerevan. Then one day an Armenian lady named Ovsanna saw him as he was searching for something to eat and drink."

Rebecca smiled. "Ovsanna. That's a pretty name. What did she do?"

"She took him in, and she cared for him."

"How old was he when she saved him?"

Grandpa scratched his chin. "I think by that time he was about five months old. And a hungry five-month-old puppy he was. He gobbled the food Miss Ovsanna gave him right down, and he drank all of the water in the bowl that she gave him."

That made Ben smile. "She gave him something to eat, something to drink, and she gave him a home. I bet little Dikran loved her right away."

Grandpa started chuckling quietly to himself. Ben and Rebecca looked at each other in confusion, and then they both looked at Grandpa. Ben spoke first. "What is so funny? Don't you think it was nice of the lady to take him in and care for him?"

Grandpa stopped chuckling and smiled at Ben. "I think what she did was wonderful. I'm laughing because you, Ben, just about perfectly quoted one of the best verses in the whole Bible. Did you catch that, Becca?"

Rebecca tilted her head in thought, then straightened up and smiled. "That's right, Grandpa. I think from Matthew, right?"

"That's right. Matthew chapter 25, verse 35."

Ben was looking back and forth at the two, shaking his head. "I didn't say anything from the Bible. I don't even read it."

Grandpa smiled and reached into one of his pockets and pulled out a worn little book. He flipped through it and stopped at a page that was more than halfway through. "Here, Ben, right where my finger is. Read those three sentences that are highlighted." It was dark, but Grandpa had the lantern, and he held it close.

Ben took the book and looked where Grandpa had put his finger. His eyes got wide as he read to himself.

Grandpa urged him on. "Ben, read it out loud so we all can hear what it says."

Ben hesitated for a moment, and then he read out loud. *"For I was hungry and you gave me something to eat, I was thirsty and you gave me something to drink, I was a stranger and you invited me in."* Ben slowly looked up at Grandpa. For one of the only times in his life, Ben didn't know what to say. He just sat there. He looked back down at the page and read the words again, this time silently. Then he looked back up at Grandpa. "Why are these sentences written in red letters?"

Grandpa smiled at Ben. "Those red letters mean that Jesus himself was the one who spoke those words."

Ben still just sat there. He was partly fascinated but also a bit uncomfortable. He had never cared about God, or Jesus, or the Bible, and this was… different. Rebecca could see the conflict in her brother, and Grandpa saw it too. He didn't want Ben to lose interest, so he picked back up with Dikran and his story. "Do you want to know what else Miss Ovsanna did when she saved Dikran? She took a picture of him."

That brought Ben back into Dikran's story. "She did? Boy, I sure would love to see that picture."

Grandpa dug into his other pocket and pulled something out. "Well, it just so happens…"

Ben and Rebecca quickly leaned forward on the bench, almost tipping it over. "You have a picture of Dikran!?"

"I do. Are you sure you want to see it? He doesn't look too good. Remember the condition he was in when Miss Ovsanna found him."

Ben was now out of his seat, filled with excitement. "Yes, Grandpa, we want to see him! Please!"

"Okay." Grandpa laughed at Ben's enthusiasm. "But first, back in your seat. Both of you can look at the same time."

Ben and Rebecca slid close to each other so they could both see Dikran. Grandpa held the picture in front of them and made sure there was enough light by holding the lantern close.

Both children gasped, but they couldn't take their eyes off of the picture. Rebecca held back a tear. "Look at his legs. And see how skinny he is. Poor Dikran."

Ben was as moved by the picture as his sister. "Grandpa, see how sad he looks? How could someone let that happen? And look, you were right. He doesn't have any ears. And it almost looks like he is walking on his elbows. This is so sad."

"It is sad, Ben." Grandpa paused, then reached into his pocket and pulled out another picture. "Can you handle another picture of Dikran?"

Ben and Rebecca both nodded their heads up and down. "Yes, Grandpa. We want to see."

Again, both children gasped. This time Ben was the first to speak.

"Grandpa, this is the worst thing I have ever seen. Look at his legs. And look at his face. Poor Dikran."

"I agree, Ben. But what is so great is that someone took him in. She gave him food, water, and a bed. And she gave him a name. Do you know why she named him Dikran? Do you think it was because he *looked* like a king?"

"No. He doesn't look like a king." He didn't look like a king, but Ben loved little Dikran anyway. "Why did she name him Dikran?"

"Because to her, he did look like a king. She was looking at him on the inside, at his spirit. He had the heart of a king, and she saw it. She felt that he was going to do great things someday."

Ben and Rebecca again looked at the picture of Dikran. They felt as sad for him as they ever had for an animal. They both felt that his story was going to get better, that he was going to be okay, but how? They wanted more. "What happened next, Grandpa?"

Grandpa drew a deep breath. "I hate to tell you this, but the rest of the story will have to wait. It's late, and I know that you both are tired. We will continue Dikran's story tomorrow."

They both gasped. "Wait? Now?" Ben couldn't believe it. Just when things were turning around for little Dikran.

"Remember the deal, Ben. Tomorrow will come soon enough." Grandpa was a strong man, and he reached forward and scooped each one of them up in his arms and gave them a hug. Then he gently set them down. "Come on, my little ones, off to bed. Your grandma and mom are probably both asleep, so let's keep it quiet."

And off they marched, Ben and Rebecca each wrapped in their blankets and Grandpa lighting the way with his lantern.

As tired as he was, Ben was having a hard time falling asleep. He was warm and cozy in his bed, covered with soft blankets. However, his mind was far from sleep. He kept thinking about Dikran, disfigured and starving, all alone, trying to find food and shelter. In his mind, he kept seeing the pictures that Grandpa had shown them. Poor little Dikran. Then he would imagine himself coming to the rescue. *I would have saved you, Dikran.* He said that to himself over and over.

Then he would picture Miss Ovsanna rescuing Dikran. And in the back of his mind, he kept hearing that Bible verse Grandpa had made him read, and he would put himself right in the middle of those three sentences. *I would have fed you, Dikran. And I would have given you something to drink. And I sure would have invited you into my home.*

With these thoughts filling his head, Ben drifted off into sleep.

Chapter 4

BEN AWOKE TO THE SMELL OF BACON. *WOW! That smells good!* He got dressed as quickly as he could. As he tied his shoes, he thought to himself, *I'm as hungry as a dog!* Then he suddenly straightened. Dikran! "Oh, my gosh!" Now he was talking to himself out loud. "How am I going to wait until nighttime for the story to continue?"

Downstairs he saw his sister finishing her plate of French toast and bacon. "Becca, why didn't you wake me up?"

"I tried, Ben. You were out cold. I said your name three times, and you didn't stir, so I let you sleep."

"But I wanted to get up early."

Ben's mom came around the corner with a cup of hot coffee in her hands. "You were very tired, Ben. You needed your sleep. How was your story last night?"

"It was great! I loved it but it's not over. I can't wait to hear more. Where is Grandpa?"

"He is in the barn. He wants to try Raider with the harness and see how he does pulling one of the carts. Becca and I are going into town with Grandma. Want to come with us or help Grandpa with Raider?" His mom smiled because she knew the answer before she had even asked.

"Are you kidding? Help Grandpa! Is he already starting?" Ben was walking toward the back door.

"Ben, get back here and eat a good breakfast! Grandpa said he would wait."

"Okay." Ben rushed back into the kitchen to get his plate. "I just don't want him to start without me."

"Don't worry. He said he would wait. And, Ben?"

"Yes, Mom?"

"Remember the rules of the story. Do not pester Grandpa with questions about the dog."

"You mean Dikran." To Ben, Dikran was not just a dog. "I don't know if I can wait."

"You will have to."

Half an hour later Rebecca, Ben's mom and his grandma were headed out in the farm car. Ben called the old station wagon that Grandma always drove the "farm car" because it just looked like the kind of car you would drive on a farm. He was heading out to the barn to help Grandpa, looking forward to watching the big horse pull the farm cart. The cart was pretty big but so was Raider.

Ben spent the entire morning helping Grandpa hook up Raider, move him out to the east pasture where the big farm cart was, hook him up to the cart, and haul the cart back to the barn. He was full of Dikran questions, but he never got a chance to try to pry information out of Grandpa. Working the big horse was tiring, and even though Grandpa did most of the really hard stuff, Ben did pull his weight. Grandpa saw to that.

It wasn't until they got back to the barn that they got a chance to relax. Almost relax. "Not yet, Ben. First we take care of Raider. Then we can rest and have some lunch. Remember, the animals can't take care of themselves. We have to always remember that."

"Okay, Grandpa." Ben moved to help Grandpa, but his mind went to Dikran. *Who was taking care of Dikran when he was starving and lost?* Thoughts like this kept popping into his mind as he helped Grandpa put Raider away.

Lunch came and went, as did the rest of the day. Doing some odd jobs around the barn, helping Grandpa move some of the cows into different pens, and a swim in the creek took them right up to supper-time. Ben hardly saw his mom or sister, but as supper drew near, everyone seemed to meet in the kitchen and dining room.

Ben was happy to see Rebecca. She also was a reminder to him that storytime was drawing near. She was happy to see her brother too, and she asked him about his day. After they talked about their adventures, Rebecca asked Ben if he had followed the story rules. "I bet you asked Grandpa questions about Dikran all day long."

Grandpa answered for Ben. "Becca, your brother didn't say one word or ask one question all day long, even though I knew where his mind was most of the time. I was very proud of him." Grandpa paused and looked at Ben and Rebecca with a smile on his face. "I forgot to tell you. We are having a guest for supper tonight."

Ben instantly wondered if the guest was going to affect storytime. "Who?"

Grandpa smiled. "Let's just say that it will be someone I think both of you have been waiting to see."

The two looked at each other and slowly broke into smiles. They spoke together. "Greg?"

"Greg. He will be here any minute, just in time for supper."

"Yay!!" Ben and Rebecca loved Greg. He was Grandpa's number one farm hand. He knew everything about every kind of farm animal, and he could fix anything. And he was so much fun.

Rebecca looked at Grandpa. "Where has Greg been? We haven't seen him at all yet."

"I let him take some time to visit with his family. He doesn't get to see them much, and they are in town for a few days."

She accepted that without a word. She and her brother didn't know that much about Greg's family, and they didn't want to pry. They were just happy to see Greg. And just like that, they heard the rumble of Greg's big pickup truck as it pulled into the driveway. As Ben and Rebecca ran out the front door, a tall, lean man climbed out of the truck. He was very tan and looked like he spent most of his life outdoors in the sun.

"Benjamin! Rebecca!" Greg always used their full names when he talked to them. "One year goes by and you are both at least a foot taller! How are you two?"

"Great, Greg! We are so happy to see you!" They talked about school, home, and the farm for a few minutes and then headed to the house.

Supper was as delicious as it had been the evening before. Grandma's beef stew was fantastic, and her cornbread had to be the best in the county. Just like the evening before, the two children ate as fast as they could without being sloppy or rude. Ben did have to stop eating for a few moments to explain to Greg how he had walked Raider halfway across the farm all by himself, even though Grandpa was right there.

Grandpa seemed like he was in a good mood. He talked with Greg about some of the new equipment they were getting ready to buy and when it was going to be delivered to the farm. Just as Ben was finishing his dinner, Greg turned the conversation to the two kids.

"I understand that you two are getting started on a week-long story. How is it so far?"

Rebecca was the first to speak up. "It's the best story ever! A true story about a dog named Dikran. It's a sad story, but I know it will get better."

"Dikran, huh? I'll bet it will have a great ending. You know how your Grandpa is with stories."

Ben pushed himself back in his chair. "I sure hope it ends well. Poor Dikran is having a rough time right now. Mom, may we clean up and get ready for the story?"

Ben's mom smiled at him. "Yes, but both of you need to go upstairs and get ready for bed first. I have a feeling that your Grandpa will have you out late tonight."

"Thanks, Mom!" Both kids started clearing their places. Before they headed upstairs, Greg called them over. "Benjamin and Rebecca. It is so good to see you! I have to run. Your grandpa keeps me pretty busy, but I will see you real soon, okay?"

Rebecca grabbed Greg by the hand. "Tomorrow?"

"We'll see. I'll try."

"Okay. See you later, Greg!" And with that, the two headed upstairs as quickly as they could.

Never before had two children been so fast at taking a bath. Before anyone could even notice that the Ben and Rebecca had gone upstairs, they came trotting down the stairs, clean and dressed for the evening down by the creek. Looking around, they saw that Greg had left.

Ben had also noticed that the master storyteller was not anywhere to be seen. "Grandpa, where are you?"

"Where do you think?" Grandpa came strolling into the dining room with the blankets and lantern. "I had a feeling you weren't going to be able to wait."

Rebecca looked into the kitchen and saw that there were no hot cocoa mugs.

Before she could say a word, Grandma spoke. "We thought you would be extra anxious to get going with the story this evening. Do you mind if I bring your cocoa down to the creek in a few minutes?"

"Not at all! Thanks, Grandma!" Both Ben and Rebecca ran over and hugged Grandma before heading out the back door. Just before getting to the door, they turned around and ran over to their mom, hugged her too, then headed down to the creek.

"There, now." Grandpa finished wrapping the blankets around his two grandkids. "All tucked in and ready?"

"Yes." They spoke as one. Ben had more to say. "Grandpa, it was so hard waiting all day. What happened to Dikran? Did Miss Ovsanna adopt him? Where is he now? How did—"

"Ben, Ben!" Grandpa held up his hand. "Hold on to your horses! All in good time." Grandpa settled into his chair, and Ben and Rebecca did the same on their bench. Grandpa cleared his throat. "Do you remember that Miss Ovsanna had taken Dikran into her home?"

"Yes."

"Well, Miss Ovsanna was actually starting a dog rescue, and I think Dikran was one of her first dogs. There are a lot of stray dogs in Armenia, and most of them don't have much of a chance. She saw poor Dikran and knew right away that she had to do something."

Rebecca had a curious look on her face. "Does that mean she wasn't going to keep Dikran? What was she going to do with him?"

Grandpa continued. "Her first thoughts were for his nutrition and his legs. She could feed him to get some weight on him, but she had no idea what to do about his legs. So she took him to see a dog doctor."

"You mean a veterinarian? They also call them vets." Ben knew a lot about dogs, and part of that was being familiar with their health needs.

"Yes, Ben. Very good." Grandpa smiled and went on. "Miss Ovsanna took Dikran to see a vet. In fact, she took him several times. They took pictures—I mean X-rays—of his legs and wrapped them with bandages trying to straighten them out." Grandpa paused, looked at his audience, and reached into his pocket.

"Pictures?" Ben was out of his seat without realizing it.

"Pictures." Grandpa laughed and pointed to the bench. "After you have your seat."

As Ben sat back down, he heard some rustling coming from the trees behind them. Ben and Rebecca whirled around to see Grandma enter the clearing with two steaming mugs of hot cocoa.

"Yum!" Rebecca was getting a little chilly, and the cocoa would take care of that.

"Thanks, Grandma!" The two took their mugs with big smiles on their faces. Grandma returned their smiles with one of her own, then headed right back to the house. She knew that they were completely engrossed in the story, and she didn't want to interrupt.

Ben looked back at Grandpa, but he was already holding up two pictures for them to see. The first one showed Dikran on a surgery table getting his legs wrapped. It looked like he was asleep.

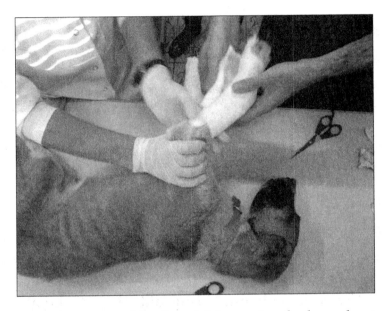

Rebecca saw his ribs sticking out as he lay asleep on the table. "Look how skinny he still is. Isn't he getting enough food?"

"It takes a while to put weight on when you are that skinny, Becca. Miss Ovsanna was doing everything that she could," Grandpa reassured her. "But it takes time. If she fed him too much, it could make him sick." Grandpa then showed them the second picture. It showed Dikran on his feet with his front legs heavily bandaged.

Ben was studying the second picture. "Grandpa, those bandages didn't make his legs straight. They are still crooked."

"That's right, Ben. The bandages didn't help."

"Why not?" Rebecca had a sad look on her face. "Why are his legs still bent?"

"They didn't know. No one did. The vets did all they could, but little Dikran's legs weren't getting better. His ribs weren't sticking out so much anymore, but his legs were still a mess."

"That's terrible!" Rebecca was quite upset. "This is a sad story, Grandpa. How sad for little Dikran."

"Don't despair, Becca. Some of the best and happiest stories start sad, but they don't end that way. Believe me, it gets better."

She smiled. "Okay, Grandpa. Tell us more."

Grandpa adjusted his chair and settled back in. "Miss Ovsanna had fallen in love with Dikran, but she was at a loss. She had no idea what to do with him, and she couldn't afford to keep taking him to the vet hospital. Whenever she got a chance, she would sit at home with Dikran in her lap and just hold him. She didn't know what else to do, and Dikran loved to be held." Grandpa smiled and dug into his pocket again, bringing out yet another picture.

Ben and Rebecca squirmed on the bench, but this time they stayed seated.

"Oh, my gosh!" Rebecca's mouth was open wide. "That is the sweetest picture I have ever seen in my whole life! He just loves her. I can tell."

Ben loved the picture as well. "Dikran looks so happy. He looks like he could stay there forever."

Grandpa agreed. "Yes he does, but that wasn't to be. Miss Ovsanna had put a picture of Dikran on the Internet, desperately hoping that someone would see it and be able to help. She didn't want to give him up, but she couldn't give him the help he needed."

Ben looked distraught. "She was going to give Dikran up? How could she do that?"

"That was the last thing she wanted to do, Ben. But she was thinking of what was best for Dikran. Sometimes the greatest act of love is to give up something that you love the most." Grandpa paused to let that sink in.

As Ben pondered what Grandpa just said, something his Sunday school teacher had said a few weeks ago popped into his head. Something about God's greatest act of love in giving up Christ for us. Ben had not understood one bit what she meant when she had said that, but what Miss Ovsanna was doing for Dikran brought just a tiny bit of understanding into his mind.

Then Ben's mind jumped back to something his new mom had told him just after he was adopted. He remembered what she said just like it was yesterday. *Ben, please don't be angry with your birth mother. She was in a very difficult situation. She didn't know what to do, and when she gave you up it was out of a love for you that can be so hard to understand.* Ben thought again about what Miss Ovsanna did for Dikran. He silently shook his head, trying to think clearly.

Finally Rebecca spoke up. "Did someone see the picture of Dikran?"

"Actually, someone did. Miss Ovsanna had reached out to the Armenian community, and an Armenian lady named Miss Laura saw his picture. She got in touch with Miss Ovsanna and told her that she would raise the money needed to fly Dikran to where she lived so she could get help for him. And would you like to guess where Miss Laura lives?"

"Where?" Ben was trying to guess in his head where it could be. He knew that there were Armenians living in America. There were even some in his class. "America?"

Grandpa smiled. "America. In Southern California."

Ben literally fell out of his seat, causing Rebecca and Grandpa to laugh out loud. "Southern California? That's where *we* live! Did Miss Laura get Dikran? Did she?"

"She did, Ben. It took a lot of money and a lot of good Armenian people in both Armenia and America to make it happen, but it did happen. Dikran came to America."

Rebecca suddenly got a sad face. "That means that Miss Ovsanna had to say 'goodbye' to him. She must have been very sad. In that picture it looks like she loves him so much."

"That is true, Becca." Even Grandpa seemed a little sad at this part of the story. "But I will tell you, this is not the end of the story. Dikran has much ahead of him." Grandpa reached into his pocket and pulled out yet another picture. "Look. Here is a picture of Dikran in his crate when he was flown to America."

By this time Ben and Rebecca were experienced at staying

on the bench when pictures came out. The picture was a close-up of Dikran's face as he peered out from the crate.

"Poor Dikran!" Rebecca was sad again. "He doesn't know what is happening."

Ben agreed. "He keeps getting bounced around. He doesn't know why."

Grandpa nodded his head in agreement. "No, he doesn't."

Ben felt sad, too. "What happened when he got to California?"

"Miss Laura took him in. She loved him, and he loved her too. They bonded to each other very quickly. And remember, there were other Armenian ladies who helped get Dikran to America. Look." Grandpa pulled another picture from his pocket. Ben and Rebecca leaned forward as Grandpa held the picture up for them to see.

"That is so cute." Rebecca had a smile on her face. "Look at Dikran with his new family."

"Yes." Grandpa nodded his head. "They called themselves 'Dikran's Aunties.' But it was Miss Laura that he lived with. That's her right there." Grandpa pointed to one of the ladies in the picture.

"Did she take Dikran to the doctor to see about fixing his legs?"

"Yes, Becca, she took him to a vet. Dikran had put on some weight, but his legs were still crooked. And the news that the vet gave her wasn't exactly what she wanted to hear."

"Oh, no!" Ben was already worried for Dikran. "What was wrong?"

"Well, there was a surgery that *might* fix Dikran's legs, but it was very expensive and would take him about one full year to recover. That meant that Dikran would have to be kept very quiet for that whole year."

Rebecca couldn't believe it. "A whole year? Wow! How was he going to do that?"

Grandpa cleared his throat. "Hold on now. There was something else going on, too. Dikran was developing what are called hygromas on his elbows. Big fluid filled sacs, like lemons, right on his elbows."

Rebecca looked horrified. "What? Why? Didn't he have enough to deal with?"

Grandpa shrugged his shoulders. "They were probably from the stress on his elbows from walking the way he did because of his deformed legs. They didn't seem to hurt him, but they were still there, and it usually takes a surgical procedure to fix them. And that's not all."

"Not all?" Ben was horrified. "What else could possibly go wrong?"

"This one is a little harder to explain. Do you know how it was that Dikran was able to survive all of the difficult challenges that he faced at so young an age?"

Ben and Rebecca looked at each other, then back to Grandpa. They both shrugged.

"He was one tough little boy, and he had a lot of energy."

Ben perked right up. "It's called drive, Grandpa! Dikran has a lot of drive! He looks so calm and sweet in those pictures, but he must have a lot of drive. Is that it?"

"That's it, Ben. In fact, Dikran had so much drive that Miss Laura was having a hard time keeping control of him. She loved him dearly, but he was a wild one! Remember that he was getting more weight on his bones, so he was feeling better. And as he felt better, he got more and more wild. He would charge around Miss Laura's house like a maniac, and her other dogs would hide from him under the bed."

Rebecca was concerned for Dikran. "Didn't it hurt his legs to charge around like that?"

Grandpa shrugged. "If it did, he never acted like it. He seemed to have too much fun charging around the house and yard."

Ben was also concerned. "What did she do? Was Dikran going to lose another home?"

"Well, Ben, Miss Laura had spent a lot of time doing volunteer work for a dog rescue organization. This rescue organization had actually helped with getting Dikran to America, and they were helping with trying to get him adopted. She called them and explained what was going on with Dikran. She told them that she felt terrible, but she was unable to give him the care he needed."

Ben's voice was quiet and sad. "What did they say?"

"They told Miss Laura about a man who was a dog trainer, and he also owned a dog boarding business. They said that they had sent many homeless dogs to him that were too wild to be adopted."

Ben didn't know if he liked this idea or not. "What would he do with them?"

"He would keep them at his kennel while he trained them. When he felt that they were ready for adoption, he would let the dog rescue people know, and they would then find homes for the dogs."

"Is that where Dikran went?" Rebecca had another question, but she wanted to know the answer to this one first.

"Miss Laura called the trainer and asked him if he could help her with a dog. He said that he would be glad to help."

Before Rebecca could ask her next question, Ben had one of his own. "But had this trainer ever trained a Gampr? I bet he hadn't even heard of a Gampr before."

Grandpa shook his head. "No, he hadn't ever heard of a Gampr. But he had been training dogs for over thirty years, including police dogs and dogs in movies. He was very experienced."

"But he hadn't ever seen a dog as special as Dikran."

Rebecca agreed, and voiced her other concern. "What about Dikran's legs? How was a dog trainer going to help his legs?"

43

"No one was sure about that one. Miss Laura just knew that she wasn't going to be able to keep him at her home. He was too much for her."

"So did she take Dikran to this trainer?"

"Yes, Ben, she did. And she was very sad to give him away. This is Miss Laura with Dikran just before she dropped him off." Grandpa pulled out another picture. It was kind of a funny picture of Miss Laura holding Dikran as he just hung in her arms.

Ben looked very closely at the picture. "He looks so happy just hanging there, close to Miss Laura."

Grandpa set the picture down. "Yes, Dikran loved her very much."

Rebecca had been looking at the picture even after Grandpa had set it down, then she looked up. "What is this trainer's name?"

"Mr. Dave. And his wife helped him run the business too. Her name is Mrs. Paula."

Ben couldn't believe Dikran's bad luck. "How sad for little Dikran. He probably thought that nobody wanted him. He just keeps getting passed around. Won't he ever find a home?"

Rebecca had another concern for Dikran. "Was he going to have to stay in a cage now? He wouldn't even be able to stay in a home with someone?"

"You two just hang on. Let's get back to the story." Grandpa paused for a moment. "Miss Laura did drop Dikran off at the kennel. And when she did, he barked at Mr. Dave. He wasn't very used to men."

Ben frowned. "Did Dikran bite him?"

"No, he didn't. Mr. Dave was very good and understanding with Dikran. He spent time with him so they could become friends. Remember that it was Mr. Dave's job to train Dikran to be a well-behaved dog so that someone would be able to adopt him. This meant that Dikran had to learn to trust him."

"But did Dikran have to live in a cage?"

"No, he didn't. He had a pretty big dog run all to himself, and Mr. Dave spent a lot of time with him every day."

"I'll bet he was the smartest dog Mr. Dave had ever trained." Ben was sure about that.

"Actually, Dikran was one of the most stubborn dogs Mr. Dave had ever seen. Gamprs aren't supposed to be household pets. They are bred to be protectors, and the instinct to look out for wolves and other threatening animals is very strong. Dikran felt that he needed to be looking out for threats all of the time, and that made it very challenging for Mr. Dave."

"So what did he do?" Rebecca was worried that Dikran wasn't going to enjoy life at the kennel.

Grandpa leaned back and stretched his legs. "He did two things. First of all, he studied and learned everything he could about Gamprs. There are very few Gamprs in America, so he went on the Internet to get information, and a lot of that information came from Armenia."

"That sounds like a good idea. You said that Mr. Dave did two things, Grandpa. What else did he do?"

"Well, Becca. Mr. Dave knew that Dikran had a lot of energy." Grandpa looked at Ben. "Drive. He had a lot of drive. So he set up a very active schedule, and made sure that everything Dikran did was with Mr. Dave. He completely controlled Dikran's entire day, each and every day."

Ben understood. He had read about this. "He did that so Dikran would look at him as the pack leader, right?"

"That's it, Ben. Very good."

"That doesn't sound very fun to me." Rebecca had a frown on her face.

"It actually was a lot of fun. Dikran got a lot more than obedience training. He got to play, he went on walks, and Mr. Dave would spend time every day just sitting with him, giving him love and attention. And he gave Dikran a new name. Not a new name, really, just a shortened version of his name. He started to call him Deke."

"Deke." Ben said the name a few more times. "I like it, but why did Mr. Dave shorten his name?"

"I think because it was an easier name to say for the obedience training. But he also kept the name Dikran. Mr. Dave always wanted to remember Dikran's history and country of birth."

"But Mr. Dave was eventually going to have to give him up?" Ben didn't like that part of the deal at all. He knew that Deke would start to love Mr. Dave the same way he had loved Miss Ovsanna and Miss Laura. And then he would be taken from Mr. Dave too. It wasn't fair at all.

"That was the plan, Ben. Mr. Dave knew that from the beginning. Just like all the other homeless dogs he had trained, Dikran would have to go."

That made Ben sad again. "But how would they know that whoever took Dikran would be able to take good care of him? And what about his legs? It just doesn't seem like there is a good answer for his problems. What happened next?"

Grandpa stood up and smiled a pretend sad smile down at Ben and Rebecca.

Rebecca grimaced in horror. "Oh, no! We *can't* stop here! We need to know what happened next!"

Ben felt the same way. "Grandpa, there is *no way* I will be able to sleep tonight. This is such a sad story for little Deke."

"I am truly sorry, my little buttercups, but look at the time! It is almost tomorrow." He scooped them both up. "Tomorrow night will come soon enough. Then you will begin to see God's amazing plan unfold for an abandoned, starved, and disfigured little runt puppy." He gave the lantern to Ben. "Your turn to light the way."

Ben held the lantern high as they walked, and he was deep in thought. "Grandpa?"

"Yes, Ben."

"Miss Ovsanna and Miss Laura really loved Dikran, didn't they?"

"Yes, they did. Very much."

"But they both still gave him up."

"Yes, Ben, they still gave him up." It seemed like Grandpa wanted Ben to figure this out on his own.

"So even though they loved him very much and were going to miss him a lot, they gave him up because they were doing what was best for Dikran? They didn't stop loving him?"

"They probably loved him even more after they decided to give him up. It can be hard to understand that until you have to do it."

Ben stopped walking. What Grandpa just said brought back to his mind what his mom had told him about his birth mother giving him up. He was looking at the ground and thinking hard when he felt a hand on his shoulder. He looked up and saw that Grandpa was kneeling on the ground, looking at him with soft eyes. "Benjamin, you weren't just tossed out like Dikran was. That was cruel, and Dikran didn't deserve that kind of treatment. What the lady who gave birth to you did was just like what Miss Ovsanna and Miss Laura did for Dikran. It was done out of love. She was in a tough situation and wanted what was best for you." Grandpa smiled at Ben and stood up. "Come on, farmer Ben. I know how tired you are."

Ben and Rebecca were both silent for the rest of the hike back to the house. They hugged Grandpa good-night and walked to the top of the stairs in silence as well. They were both deep in thought, each wondering what was going to happen to little Deke.

At the top of the stairs, Ben turned to his sister, his voice a quiet whisper. "Grandpa said something about God's plan. Deke is such a poor little puppy. How could a kind God have anything to do with this story?"

"Ben." Rebecca put both of her hands on Ben's shoulders. "Look at you. You know, after I was born, Mom had some medical problems. She prayed to God for years for another child, and for a long time she thought that God wasn't listening, that He didn't have a plan for her."

Ben thought about how hard it was for him before becoming part of this family. All he could remember was being in and out of foster homes and staying at the orphanage. That was a life that he hated. All he had wanted was a family.

Rebecca continued. "After I was born Mom really wanted a son. She prayed to God every day, and sometimes I even prayed with her. And then we found out about you. The day we adopted you was one of the happiest days of her life." She smiled a big smile. "Mine too. No one knew how all of that was going to happen, but it did. And look at you now. You are part of our family. That is what Grandpa means when he talks about God's plan. Having you become part our family was God's plan. We don't know yet how Dikran's story ends, but God does."

Ben didn't know what to say, so he just stood there looking at his sister. After a moment, Rebecca gave him a hug, said goodnight, and headed to her room. Ben stood there for a full minute, then slowly turned and headed to his room.

Chapter 5

BEN WOKE UP ON HIS OWN, FEELING WELL rested. He had slept straight through the night, but it had taken him a while to fall asleep. Dikran's story kept swirling around in his head. For the first time since the story began, he started to very clearly see some of his own life in the story of Dikran. They were both runts, and they had both been without a family. Maybe that was why he felt so strongly about little Deke.

You were small and disfigured and they just threw you out. This thought kept going through Ben's head as he got dressed. Then he thought about what Grandpa had said about God's plan. He shook his head. *How could God have a plan for a little runt Gampr?* Then he thought about what his mom and grandpa had said about his birth mother, and another question just popped into his head. *How could God have a plan for a little runt boy?*

As he pushed these thoughts out of his head, still another thought jumped right in, that of Rebecca standing there with her hands on his shoulders last night telling him that he was part of her family. As he was thinking this, a warm feeling came over him as he felt that maybe he really did belong.

His thoughts then went back to Dikran, and he felt sad again. Poor Dikran didn't belong to anyone. He was sure that the story was going to end well because Grandpa never told stories that ended sad, but how would it get better? Miss Ovsanna felt that there were great things in Dikran's future, but what great things could a crippled little runt be capable of? In order for *that* to happen, he would need some serious help. Major help, like help from... *God?*

Ben shook his head and spoke out loud. "Earth calling Ben!" He made his bed, got dressed, and headed down for breakfast. He met his sister at the top of the stairs. Rebecca spoke first. "You are up early. Did you sleep well?"

"I slept okay, but I couldn't get Dikran out of my head. He is such a poor boy. I can't wait for tonight. This waiting each day is like torture."

"Same here. He really is a poor boy. But the story *must* have a happy ending! I wonder what we're doing today."

Right as they got to the bottom of the stairs, Grandma came walking out of the kitchen with two plates of pancakes, bacon, and scrambled eggs.

"Wow, Grandma! You are the best!" Ben had been so preoccupied with Dikran, he hadn't realized how hungry he was. "Do you know what we are doing today?"

"There are some big dead trees out in the west pasture that your grandpa is taking down today."

"That sounds cool! Can I help?"

Grandma patted his shoulder. "I think they just might need your strong back and shoulders."

Ben thought about what Grandma had just said. "They?"

Grandma nodded. "Greg and some of the other farmhands are out there. I think they are going to use Raider to haul the trees out of the pasture once they are down. Your grandpa said something about needing someone to help work Raider."

"Awesome! I can handle Raider! Maybe Grandpa will let me."

Grandma laughed. "Maybe, but not until you have a good breakfast."

"What about Becca?"

Grandma smiled. "Rebecca will be helping your mother and me with some cooking and baking today. We are having company for supper."

Ben frowned. "Company?" This could seriously affect storytime.

Grandma seemed to read his mind. "Don't worry, Ben. Supper will be early. Grandpa doesn't plan on missing out on the story."

That satisfied Ben. He looked at his loaded plate and dug in.

Taking down the big trees was quite a chore, but with five of them working, they had them down by lunchtime. Ben thought it was really neat watching the trees come crashing down. Right before each tree came down, Ben's mom came out with her camera to film the event. After the last tree, the women brought out lunch, saying that the men were all too dirty to come into the house to eat.

Ben enjoyed the day because he felt like he was one of the men. He worked hard, and as lunch was ending, Grandpa asked him to help get Raider ready.

Ben eagerly jumped to his feet. They got Raider's harness on, and Ben got to walk him to the pasture and position him so they could hook up the tree branches.

As Grandpa and Ben had been preparing Raider, Greg and the other men were using big chainsaws to cut the trees into sizes that Raider could haul. It took three hours for the trees to get hauled over to a big clearing next to the barn. Everyone was impressed with how strong Raider was. They all congratulated Grandpa on getting such a fine horse.

"We will leave all these branches here for now." Grandpa explained to Ben that over the next several weeks they would cut up most of the branches for firewood. Ben was exhausted as they put Raider away. He had never worked so hard in his life, and he was pleased when they all headed down to the creek to jump in and clean themselves the fun way.

"Grandpa, who is the company that is coming over for supper?" Ben was already thinking ahead to storytime.

Grandpa smiled and pointed at the men who were jumping into the creek. "My hardworking crew. Their families should be here any time now so let's get cleaned up. We don't want to delay supper, do we?" Grandpa winked at Ben as he finished speaking.

"No, we don't!" Without any further delay, Ben leaped into the cool, refreshing water.

Supper had been fun, and Ben really felt like one of the men. Several times during the dinner conversation, someone would comment on how hard Ben had worked and how good he was with Raider. Ben felt warm inside, and he knew it was more than Grandma's good cooking that made him feel that way.

When supper and dessert were done, all the folks started to leave. Tomorrow was a workday, and up here in farmland people started work early. That meant early to bed. Greg was the last to leave. He had been talking quietly with Grandpa for the last part of dinner. He got up, told the women how delicious the meal had been, and walked over to Ben.

"I need to get going, Ben, and I'm not sure if I will be here tomorrow. Enjoy the story tonight."

"Thanks, Greg. This is the best story I have ever heard, but there are a lot of sad parts too."

"Well, I'm sure everything is going to work out for little Deke. See you later."

Goodbyes were said, and Greg headed out the door. Ben said bye to Greg, but something was nagging at the back of his mind. Something that Greg had said, but Ben couldn't figure out what it was. He spent a minute thinking about what it could be, then shook his head and got up to help clear the table.

Ten minutes later, Ben and his sister were sitting on the story bench. Wrapped in their blankets and sipping their hot cocoa, the two of them looked expectantly at Grandpa.

Grandpa smiled back at them. "Do you remember where we left off?"

Ben spoke right up. "Mr. Dave was training Deke and spending a lot of time with him. Was Deke starting to love Mr. Dave?"

"Yes, he was. In fact, before every training session, Mr. Dave would take Deke to the training area, sit down in a chair, and just give Deke some loving. And

Deke started loving him right back. Look. Deke would always end up on Mr. Dave's lap." Grandpa reached into his pocket and pulled out a picture.

Rebecca loved the picture. "Look how happy Dikran is. You can tell. Mr. Dave looks happy too. It looks like they love each other."

Ben stared at the picture for a long moment, then looked up. "Grandpa, where did you get all of these pictures? How do you know so much about Dikran's life?"

"Now, Ben. You know that you can't ask me that. You just enjoy the story. Maybe when it's over you can ask me those questions, but not now."

"Okay." Ben looked back at the picture. "Deke sure wants a family, doesn't he?"

"Yes, he does. Now, as his training went along, Dikran started to fall into the routine. He started to learn what Mr. Dave was teaching him, and he absolutely loved his play sessions. His days were full of fun. The only part he didn't like was when Mr. Dave and his wife went to their own home at the end of each day. He would sleep in his dog run at night and wish he had a family of his own."

Rebecca sniffled. "Is Dikran there right now, all by himself?"

Grandpa hesitated as he looked at his two sad grandkids. "No, he isn't. But don't get ahead of the story."

Ben answered. "Okay." They both were happy with the answer.

Grandpa went on. "There is something else that Mr. Dave started doing. At the end of each day he would sit with little Deke and massage his front legs. He would also gently stretch his feet like he was trying to straighten them out."

"Oh, wow!" Rebecca didn't know about that. "Didn't that hurt his legs? Did he try to bite Mr. Dave?"

"Deke never tried to bite him, but at first he wasn't very happy about having his legs touched. He would try to pull them away."

"Did that make Mr. Dave stop?"

"No, Ben, he didn't stop. And then Dikran began to trust Mr. Dave. It didn't take long for Deke to look forward to his leg rubs. Soon he liked it so much that he would lie on his side, hold one of his legs out to Mr. Dave, and fall asleep as he was getting his treatment."

"That is so sweet! I bet he was really starting to love Mr. Dave."

"Yes he was, Becca. And Mr. Dave's wife started putting fresh blankets in Deke's dog run every day so his poor elbows wouldn't have to be on the hard concrete every time he would lie down. And they put a dog bed in with him as well. Look at Dikran after one of his exercise sessions. Mr. Dave would really tire him out." Again, Grandpa dug into his pocket and pulled out a picture.

Ben and Rebecca laughed out loud at the sight of Dikran asleep in his run, legs pointed in every which direction. "Wow!" Ben liked this part. "Deke is getting treated like a prince. Did the leg rubs help at all?"

"No one can say for sure if the blankets and leg rubs helped, but do you want to know what started to happen?"

Ben leaned forward. "What?"

His legs were slowly starting to straighten, and the hygromas on his elbows were getting smaller."

Ben was out of his seat. "Really? For real?"

"For real, Ben. And he had no surgery or medical treatment at all. Look at how his legs are starting to get better."

Ben and Rebecca stared at the picture. Ben was still on his feet, his mouth hanging open. "No surgery? For real? Grandpa, that's like a miracle! A miracle for Dikran!" Ben stopped and stood there, realizing what he had just said.

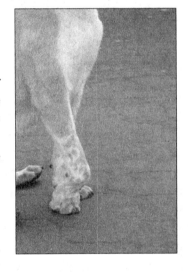

"Yes, Ben, it was like a miracle for Dikran. And there was more to come. This was just the start."

Rebecca had a big smile on her face. "How great for little Dikran. What happened next?"

Ben was back in his seat as Grandpa continued. "Dikran was starting to learn more and more. He was a strong-willed little boy, but he was smart as a whip, too."

"I told you he was smart." Ben loved the way the story was going. "The smartest of all."

"He was smart. Mr. Dave was doing some new things with his training, and Deke was starting to do some tricks too."

"Oh, wow!" Ben was on his feet again. "Deke was like a star."

Grandpa agreed. "And guess what happened next? Miss Laura and the rest of Dikran's Aunties came to visit him. They had heard about how well he was doing, and they wanted to see him."

"Yay!" Rebecca loved that idea. "Dikran would love to see his Aunties, especially Miss Laura."

"Well, they did come to visit him, and Dikran really loved seeing them." Grandpa smiled at Rebecca. "Especially Miss Laura. He got super excited when he saw her. And then Mr. Dave showed off how smart Dikran was and how much he had learned."

"I bet they were all impressed." Rebecca was sure of that.

"They were." Grandpa hesitated for a moment before continuing. "But that wasn't all. Miss Laura talked to Mr. Dave. She told him that she thought he should adopt Dikran. She told him that they were perfect for each other, and that she didn't think that anyone else was going to be able to handle Dikran. He was a small boy, but he was so energetic and strong willed that he needed Mr. Dave."

Ben agreed. "What did Mr. Dave say?"

"Not much. Mr. Dave and his wife already had three dogs, and two of them had been adopted after having rough starts in life themselves. Their son John was in high school, and with his activities and the three dogs, their lives were quite busy."

Rebecca protested. "But Dikran loved Mr. Dave."

"Yes he did, and with every passing day, something was happening to Mr. Dave. He was becoming more and more attached to Deke, and Deke was becoming more attached to Mr. Dave. Deke was very different from any dog Mr. Dave had ever worked with, but he was so special, and he loved Mr. Dave so much."

Ben looked upset when he heard this. "Is Deke going to have to leave Mr. Dave too? That would be the worst thing I have ever heard of."

Grandpa leaned back in his chair, looking back and forth from Ben to Rebecca. "Not many days later, Mr. Dave walked up to his wife and told her that he was really falling in love with Dikran, and that he didn't think that he would be able to give him up."

Rebecca had a look of excitement on her face. "Really? What did she say?"

"Mrs. Paula knew her husband well. After all, they had been married for about twenty-five years at that time. She knew that Mr. Dave loved Deke, and she did too. Their lives were already quite busy, but she agreed that no one else was going to be able to give Dikran what he needed. So guess what?"

"What? Did they actually adopt him?" Ben was on the very edge of his seat.

Grandpa smiled. "They made it official and actually adopted him."

"Whoopee!!" Ben and Rebecca both jumped off of the bench and cheered. "Dikran finally has a home! The best home!"

"Yes, he does. And guess what else?"

Both kids were still on their feet. "What?"

"Dikran's legs were now completely straight and the hygromas on his elbows were all gone. He was healed!" Grandpa pulled out another picture, one that he had been excited about showing to Ben and Rebecca. They quickly sat back down and leaned forward as Grandpa held the picture and lantern close.

"Yippie! Hooray!" They jumped up in joy. "Dikran has a home, and he is healed! This is the best story ever!"

The two sat back on the bench. Ben was now looking very thoughtful. "Grandpa, really, how did Dikran's legs heal? They were so crooked before, and now they look perfect."

"Ben, what do you think? He was never treated medically at all. But before I answer that question, wait for the rest of the story. We aren't done. There is still much that is going to happen in Dikran's life."

"More?" Rebecca was excited. "You mean this isn't the end?"

"In some ways, my dear, this is just the beginning. I told you on the first night that this was unlike any story you have ever heard. Dikran has much ahead of him."

"Wow! What more could there be?"

"You will be surprised how much more there is to this story. But, first, back to his new home. It wasn't that easy at first. Remember that Mr. Dave and Mrs. Paula had three other dogs. And even though all three were all quite a bit bigger than Dikran, he felt that they were all his new play toys, just like Miss Laura's dogs had been. Dikran wanted to charge around and play with his new packmates, and he would play quite rough."

Ben could see the potential problem with that. "Did Mr. Dave's dogs accept Dikran right away, or did they not like him?"

"Earlier I had told you that two of their dogs were rescued, just like Dikran. One of them was a German shepherd named Greta, and the other was Jackie, a Belgian Malinois. Do you know that breed, Ben?"

"I sure do, Grandpa. They are used a lot for police dogs. I read about them right before summer vacation started. They are really fast."

"Yes, they are. And Jackie had been abandoned, too, just like Dikran, but here in California. She had some trust issues, and she didn't like Dikran."

"So what did Mr. Dave do?"

"When Dikran came to their home, there were plenty of rules. Deke was kept on a leash in the house so he wouldn't pester the other dogs, especially Jackie. And whenever they went out to play, each dog would have their own toy." Grandpa smiled and once more reached into his pocket. "Here is Dikran with Jackie and Greta after a play session."

"Oh, my goodness! They are so beautiful!" Rebecca pointed to the darker of the three dogs. "Is that Greta?"

"Yes. She was also rescued from the streets."

"How wonderful! All three saved, and now they are a family."

"A pack." Ben corrected his sister. "Grandpa? You said that they already had three dogs before they adopted Dikran. So now they have four. Where is the fourth dog?"

"That is very observant of you, Ben. The fourth dog was a big boy German shepherd named Titus. He was quite old by this time, and he stayed home when the three youngsters went to the park to play."

"Titus." Rebecca said the name slowly. "There is a book in the Bible named 'Titus.'"

"That is right." Grandpa nodded his approval. "That is who Mr. Dave named him after."

Ben was really pleased with the way the story was going. "So now Dikran had his for-real home, right?"

Grandpa nodded his head. "Right. And he loved his new home very much. It didn't take long for Titus,

Greta, and Jackie to love him too. And remember, Mr. Dave and Mrs. Paula had a son who was in high school. His name was John. Deke loved John, and John loved Deke right back."

"Wow!" Ben thought that was great. "John was so lucky. What a great story, Grandpa!"

"It is a great story, but Dikran's story with his new family was just getting started. You will hardly believe what is in store for him!" Before Ben or Rebecca had a chance to say a word, Grandpa stood up with that smile of his and stretched his arms and legs.

"Oh, no!" The two protested, but not too much. It was late, and they were both quite tired. They let Grandpa scoop them out of their bench and even let him carry them halfway back to the house.

"Grandpa, this is the best story of all time. I can't wait to see what is next for Dikran."

"I guarantee that you will love it. Now off to bed, both of you."

At the top of the stairs Rebecca touched Ben on the shoulder. She smiled at her brother. "Do you still think God has nothing to do with this story? Did you see how great Dikran looked in those pictures? How do you think that happened?"

Ben looked at his sister. He didn't say a word out loud, but to himself he wondered the same thing. *How did that happen?*

Rebecca was already headed to her room. "Good night, Ben."

"Good night, Becca." Ben turned and walked to his room, thinking about Deke's transformation. *How did that happen? Really?* He couldn't help but remember what Grandpa had said last night about "God's plan." And as he climbed into bed, another thought formed in his mind. *It sure seemed like Mr. Dave and his family were the right place for Dikran. And he never would have gotten to Mr. Dave if Miss Laura hadn't gotten him. And he never would have gotten to Miss Laura if Miss Ovsanna…* And with these thoughts going through Ben's tired mind, he drifted into a deep and restful sleep.

Chapter 6

BEN SLEPT THE WHOLE NIGHT WITHOUT waking up, and he had a dream that was so realistic, he thought it was really happening. He dreamed that Dikran got lost in the mountains and no one could find him. Then Ben was in those same mountains, looking for Deke. He kept saying to himself that he would feed him, give him something to drink, and take him into his own home. And then Greg was up there helping him. "Deke! Deke!" Greg was calling him, over and over. As the sun was setting, they could hear the coyotes howling, and they still couldn't find him. Then, right in the middle of it, Ben woke up to find that morning had arrived.

"Ben! Wake up!" Ben heard his mom's voice as she called him and knocked on the door.

"I'm up, Mom."

"Hurry up, dear. We are going into town as soon as breakfast is over. You are coming with us."

Ben frowned. "Can't I stay here with Grandpa?"

"Grandpa is going too. There is an auction, and he is going to look at some cows." Ben's mom jiggled the door. "Hurry up. Grandpa wants to get there before all the good cows are gone."

"On my way, Mom!" Going into town to buy groceries was boring, but looking at cows was fun. Ben was on his way downstairs in a flash. Once in the dining room, he noticed that he was… again… the last one to eat.

Grandpa was just finishing up. "Did you sleep well, Ben?"

"Yes, but I kept dreaming that Dikran was lost in the mountains."

"Well, we're glad it was just a dream." Grandpa grinned at Ben. "Hurry up with that French toast, Bucko. We don't want to leave you behind."

"Dad!" Ben's mom pretended to be stern. "Let Ben eat in peace."

"Oh, he knows that we aren't going anywhere without him."

Half an hour later Ben, his grandparents, his mom, and his sister were all piled into the farm car heading into town. It was an old-fashioned station wagon with the bench seat way in the rear that faced backwards. Ben and Rebecca had this seat, and it was really fun facing backwards and looking at things as they zipped by.

Rebecca looked at her brother. "That sounds like a terrible dream you had last night about Dikran getting lost."

"It was." Ben shuddered as he thought about poor Dikran, lost in the mountains. "I kept looking for him, but I couldn't find him."

"Did you get lost, too?"

"No. Greg was with me, and he kept yelling."

"Yelling?" Rebecca laughed. "What was he yelling?"

"He was just yelling for Deke. He was yelling his name over and over."

"Does Greg even know about Dikran?" Rebecca thought for a moment, and then answered her own question. "Oh, yes. We told him at dinner."

"Right. A couple of nights ago I think I told him about the story, just before we went down to the creek. And last night I remember he said…" Ben paused and looked off into the distance. Something was bothering him, and he was thinking hard.

Rebecca knew Ben was trying to figure something out. "What is it, Ben? What did Greg say?"

Ben thought for a moment more. "He said that he was sure that everything was going to work out for… Deke." Ben wrinkled his forehead.

"What is wrong with that?"

"Because I never told Greg that his name was Deke. I only said 'Dikran.' How did he know his name was Deke?"

Rebecca smiled. She thought it was funny whenever her brother tried to be a detective. "Silly, Grandpa probably told him."

Ben thought about that. He turned in his seat. "Grandpa!" He had to practically yell because Grandpa was way up front in the driver's seat.

"Yes, Ben?"

"Have you said anything to Greg about our story?"

Grandpa was silent for a moment as he thought. "No, I haven't said a word. Why?"

"Nothing, Grandpa. Thanks." Ben turned and looked at his sister with an "I told you so" look. Rebecca just shrugged her shoulders.

Ben folded his arms and frowned to himself as he tried to figure the mystery out. He was still deep in thought as they pulled into town.

The day had been fun, and it went by fast. Grandpa bought five new cows and told everyone that he would have them picked up tomorrow. They went to the hardware store for a few supplies, and Ben's grandma, mom, and sister went to the department store for some material and sewing supplies.

"If we throw out clothing every time something gets a little tear, we would be buying new clothes every day!" Even though the farm was successful, Grandma was very careful with their money.

As suppertime drew near, they were still in town. This caused Ben to worry about storytime. He was thinking silently. *By the time we get home it will be late, and Grandma hasn't even started cooking.* He was getting more and more worried as he kept thinking about the story when he felt Grandpa touch him on his shoulder.

"Stop worrying, Ben. Look."

Ben looked to where Grandpa was pointing. There was a big neon sign that said "COUNTRY DINER."

Grandpa grinned down at Ben. "We are eating out tonight so we won't miss storytime."

"Yay!" Ben was instantly excited. He didn't think he could miss a night of Dikran's story.

"Yay?" Grandma looked at Ben with a stern face. "Are you saying that you would rather eat the food here instead of what I cook?"

At first, Ben thought Grandma was serious, but she couldn't hide her smile any longer. She had been teasing him. The whole family knew that Ben could hardly wait to get down to the creek.

Dinner had been good, but not the same as Grandma's home cooking. Still, it had been a great way to end a busy day in town. The drive back to the farm was uneventful and relaxing. The only part that was hard was waiting to get back.

Everyone was a bit tired, so there was not much conversation on the drive. The only time Ben spoke was when they were almost home.

"Grandpa?"

"Yes, Ben?"

"Will Greg be at the farm when we get there?"

Grandpa shook his head. "I don't think so. He is with his family right now. He may be at the farm for a bit tomorrow, though. Everything okay?"

"Yes." Ben leaned back in his seat and relaxed for the rest of the trip. As soon as the wagon pulled into the driveway and stopped, Ben and Rebecca each grabbed some of the stuff they had purchased in town and quickly headed for the front door. The adults all laughed, and Ben could hear Grandpa's voice. "I guess this means I should hurry up. Storytime will not wait!"

Ten minutes and two world-record baths later, "B & B" — as Grandpa would sometimes call them — were in the kitchen, wrapped in their blankets, and waiting for Grandpa and their two mugs of hot cocoa. Two more minutes, mugs in hand and Grandpa leading the way with his lantern, the trio headed down to the creek.

Once they were settled in, Grandpa sat down and looked at them. "Same question that I ask every night. Do you remember where we left off?"

"I do!" Ben was the first to respond. "Dikran had a home and a family, and he was all healed."

Rebecca had a little to add. "He seemed to have found a happy ending. But you said that there was more."

Grandpa nodded. "Yes, there is quite a bit more. Deke had just experienced an amazing story of survival, healing, and finding a home. But as dramatic as all of that was, those experiences happened in order to prepare him for a bigger story. A much bigger story that is quite wonderful."

"But Grandpa." Ben was a bit confused. "How could a bad life like Dikran had prepare him for something good?"

Grandpa smiled and reached out to pat Ben on the head. "That is one of the most difficult things in life to understand. I could try to explain it, but I think that the rest of Dikran's story will help you understand that truth better than I ever could. I promise you, God really did have a plan for this little runt." Grandpa leaned back in his chair. "Like I said last night, Deke finally had a home. A home with three other dogs, and even though Titus was getting old and didn't need as much exercise, Dikran and his two new sisters needed a lot."

"That must have been hard for Mr. Dave and Mrs. Paula."

"It was, Becca. But all three dogs got a lot of attention. And little Dikran was presenting his new owners with quite a challenge. He was very different from the other dogs. Gamprs aren't really supposed to be pets. They have a lot of very strong instincts. They want to protect, they're always on the lookout for threats, and they are used to acting on their own. These qualities make them great guardians, but not always the easiest pets."

Ben looked concerned. "So what did Mr. Dave do?"

Grandpa smiled. "It was Dikran's super high energy level and his desire to be such a strong protector that made Mr. Dave begin training him in a different way than he had trained other dogs. Dikran was also very active in his mind. He was always trying to figure things out. Guardians are supposed to be independent thinkers, and Dikran was all of that."

"He was being a Gampr." Ben was proud of "his" little Gampr. "So how did Mr. Dave train him?"

"He knew that he had to let Dikran have an outlet for all of his boundless energy, so Mr. Dave began to use Deke's energy as part of his training. He also knew how active Deke's mind was, so he began to make Deke figure things out as part of his training as well."

Rebecca tilted her head. "How did he do that?"

"Mr. Dave started teaching Deke more tricks, and he did a lot of play in his training sessions, like tug-o-war and chase the toy. He mixed these things together in Deke's sessions. It gave him a great outlet for his boundless energy and made him think and be obedient at the same time. The more Deke learned, the more Mr. Dave would teach him." Grandpa smiled and dug into his pocket. "I wonder if anyone around here would like to see some pictures of Dikran doing tricks?"

"Are you kidding?" Ben was out of his seat with a jump, but he sat right back down.

Grandpa had three pictures, and he showed them to Ben and Rebecca one at a time. The first picture showed Deke jumping through a hoop that Mr. Dave was holding.

"Wow! Look at Deke sailing through the air!" Ben was very impressed. "It looks like it is so easy for him. What a strong jumper!"

Rebecca was equally impressed. "He has such good aim. That hoop isn't too big, but Dikran is flying right through it!"

"Yes, he is." Grandpa then held up a picture of Deke up on a platform sitting up like a prairie dog.

Rebecca loved the picture. "Aww, he looks so cute! Look at him just sitting there."

Ben was studying the picture closely. "Grandpa, it looks like Mr. Dave is giving Deke a hand signal. Is that right?"

"That's right, Ben. Deke had learned a lot of hand signals and a lot of balancing skills, too. Look at this one." Grandpa held the third picture up.

"How cool! Deke is standing up on his hind legs!" Ben looked a bit more closely at the last two pictures. "Grandpa, is Deke doing shows in these pictures? There are a lot of kids watching."

"Now don't get ahead of me, Ben. Just stay with the story."

"Deke looks like he is having so much fun, Grandpa." Rebecca had a question. "But how does this fit into God's plan?"

Grandpa smiled. "We are getting to that right now." Then Grandpa looked at Ben. "And we are answering your question about shows too. Mr. Dave would take Deke to different places to train because he wanted Deke to get used to training in different locations. And people were starting to notice. They would stop and ask questions, and since Deke looked so different, they would ask what kind of dog he was and where he was from. When people heard Deke's story, they would be amazed. It wasn't long before Mr. Dave was asked if he would do a show for some students at the local high school."

Rebecca was impressed. "Poor little Dikran is now a star doing shows. How grand is that?"

Ben was a little confused. "What kind of show did he do?"

"First, Mr. Dave talked about Dikran's past. He showed some pictures of Dikran in Armenia, then he brought Deke out and let everyone see how he looks now. And then he showed off Deke's training."

Rebecca thought that was a great idea. "I bet they loved him." She looked at the pictures Grandpa had just showed them. "Did he do more shows?"

Grandpa smiled. "He sure did! As word spread, Deke started to do more shows. Those last two pictures were taken at two different schools where Deke performed. He was becoming a star."

Ben loved the idea of Deke doing shows, but he was still a little confused. "So is that what God's plan was for Deke? Doing shows at schools?"

Grandpa slowly shook his head. "Not really. Doing these shows was helping to prepare Deke for what was to come. The shows were preparing Mr. Dave too."

"Prepare them for what?"

"Something that was taking root in Mr. Dave's heart. Something he felt he needed to do."

"What, Grandpa?" Ben really wanted to know what this big plan was for his little Dikran. "And what does it mean when something takes root in your heart?"

"Ben." Grandpa put his hand on Ben's shoulder and looked earnestly into his eyes. "Sometimes, when God wants you to do something, He puts things into your head and heart. Things like ideas, thoughts, or a strong desire. He started doing this to Mr. Dave."

Rebecca felt like she understood what Grandpa was saying. "What was God putting into Mr. Dave's heart?"

"There were several different things that were all coming together. The first thing was something we have already talked about. Ben, do you remember that verse from the book of Matthew?"

"You mean about being hungry and thirsty? And getting invited in?"

"Exactly!" Grandpa went on. "Mr. Dave saw that Bible verse from Matthew in the way that Deke's life began. Also, there was a connection between Deke's full name and one of the names of Jesus. Can either one of you tell me what it is?"

Ben and Rebecca sat silently, thinking hard. Neither could find the connection.

Grandpa answered for them. "Our Dikran has the name of a great king, but he came into the world as a poor little runt."

Rebecca lit up and finished the answer. "Everyone expected the Messiah to come as a great king, but He came as a poor babe. Just like Dikran."

"Yes!" Grandpa glanced at Ben. "It was obvious to Mr. Dave that Dikran's life was starting to take on a bigger meaning. Then he started to see Bible verses in each trick that Dikran learned."

"Bible verses in a trick? What verse did Mr. Dave see when Deke would jump through the hoop?"

Grandpa was ready for this. He reached into his pocket and pulled out his small, worn Bible. He handed it to Rebecca and raised his lantern. "Becca, turn to the book of Isaiah, chapter 40." He waited until she looked up at him. "Verse 31. Read it out loud when you have found it."

With Ben looking over her shoulder, Rebecca found the verse and put her finger on it.

"… *but those who hope in the Lord will renew their strength. They will soar on wings like eagles; they will run and not grow weary, they will walk and not be faint.*"

They both looked at another picture that Grandpa was holding, then Ben looked up. "Grandpa, that's Deke! He is soaring like he has wings!"

Rebecca agreed. "He sure is."

Grandpa nodded his head. "Yes. And this was happening with every trick that Mr. Dave taught Deke."

Ben wanted more. "What about the trick where Deke sits up like a prairie dog? What verse fits that one?"

Grandpa thought for a second. "Becca, turn to the book of Psalms, chapter 63. Mr. Dave calls that trick 'Sit Pretty.'" When Rebecca looked up at Grandpa, he said, "Verse 4." With Ben again looking over her shoulder, she read the verse.

"I will praise you as long as I live, and in your name I will lift up my hands."

Again, they both looked at a picture that Grandpa was showing them. Ben was again the first to speak. "Wow! Just like Deke! That's really cool, Grandpa."

Grandpa nodded. "It really is cool, Ben. And there is a lot more. It seemed like everything about

Deke's life had a verse or story in the Bible that fit right with it."

Rebecca was deep in thought. Then she suddenly looked up with a smile on her face. "I just thought of another connection between Dikran and the Bible!"

"What?" Ben was eager to know. "What connection?"

"Deke is a guardian. He protects the sheep. Jesus does the same thing for us, right, Grandpa? He watches over us."

"Wow!" Grandpa was impressed. "You do know your Bible. That is in the tenth chapter of the Gospel of John. Mr. Dave talks about that too."

Ben looked at his sister. "You *do* know about the Bible, don't you?"

She just smiled as Grandpa went on. "Mr. Dave noticed that, when these verses and stories were demonstrated by Dikran, people would really pay attention and remember them. He also noticed that people would identify with Dikran and his story."

Ben wrinkled his forehead. "Identify? What does that mean?"

Grandpa smiled. "You tell me, Ben. I don't think you remember too much from your Sunday school classes, but you sure remembered that verse from the Book of Matthew. Why do you think that is?"

That was a lot for Ben to think about. He struggled to come up with an answer.

Grandpa prodded. "Why is Deke's story so important to you? Why do you feel so strongly about him?"

Ben thought for another moment. "I think because he had such a bad start in life. He almost died, and now he is doing so well. Is that it?"

"That's part of it, Ben. Keep going. What about your own life? Was your life anything like Deke's?"

Ben hesitated. Rebecca was watching her brother closely, and she thought she saw a tear fall from one of his eyes. Then Ben slowly spoke. "Because I was just like Deke. I needed a home just like he did. I thought nobody wanted me, just like Deke probably thought that nobody wanted him." He looked up at Grandpa, and Rebecca saw that there *were* tears in his eyes.

Grandpa leaned forward and put his big hands on Ben's shoulders. His voice was very soft when he spoke. "But look at you now, Benjamin. Just like Dikran, you have a home. Your mom and sister fed you, they gave you something to drink, and they took you in. And they love you. That is why all of that bad stuff happened to Dikran. You can look at his life and see what God is doing through him. Then you can see what God is capable of doing in other people's lives. Even in the life of a black-haired little boy in California. That is what it means to identify with something. That is why you remember that verse. And do you know what else?"

Ben sniffled and wiped his eyes. "What, Grandpa?"

"The Bible actually tells us how much God cares for us. As much as He cares for the animals, He cares even more for a boy at a farm, by a creek, in the middle of California." Grandpa smiled as he said the last part.

"Where does it say that?"

"Rebecca, turn to the Gospel of Luke, and find chapter 12." Grandpa smiled at Ben. "I'll show you exactly where it says that."

A moment passed. "Found it, Grandpa. What verse?"

"Verses 6 and 7. Read it to us, dear."

Rebecca found the verse, and once again Ben was leaning over her shoulder. *"Are not five sparrows sold for two pennies? Yet not one of them is forgotten by God. Indeed, the very hairs of your head are all numbered. Don't be afraid; you are worth more than many sparrows."*

Ben giggled and looked at Grandpa. "Deke is not a sparrow."

Rebecca playfully elbowed her brother. "Don't be silly. You know what that means. God loves the animals, but He *really* loves you."

Ben looked up at Grandpa. "Is that really true?"

"It really is, Ben. Look at all you have. You are surrounded by people who love you."

"What about my new father? He didn't love me. He just left."

"He didn't leave because of you, Ben. He already had his own problems that he was dealing with. Some people just aren't ready for some of the responsibilities of life. It really had nothing to do with you." Grandpa smiled at Ben. "Life is a lot like a test. Look at all of the tests that Dikran faced. He had many difficult challenges, but did he let them stop him? Or did he just keep his eyes fixed on what was to come?"

"He just kept on going." Ben paused to think about how this story meant so much to him. "And what about now, Grandpa? What was next for Deke?"

Grandpa drew a deep breath and sighed. As he did, he looked at his watch. "Do I have to tell you what time it is?"

"Oh, no!! Not now! Please?"

"By the time you get to bed it will already be tomorrow. It has been a long day and you need your sleep. And I promise you that tomorrow night will be here before you know it."

"But, Grandpa!" Ben wasn't done trying. "Tomorrow night is our last night here. We have to be able to finish the story!"

"And finish it we will. We are almost done." Grandpa stood up and scooped the two out of the bench. "B and B, I love you both."

"We love you too, Grandpa!"

At the top of the stairs Ben turned to his sister. His voice was a quiet whisper. "Isn't this the greatest story you have ever heard? I'm so happy for little Dikran. No more 'poor Dikran.'"

Rebecca nodded and whispered back. "Yes, it is a great story. And Grandpa is right. You have a lot in common with Dikran. You two are the same, and God wants to use both of you. Good night, little brother." Rebecca gave Ben a quick hug and headed to her room.

Once again, Ben stood there silently for a minute, deep in thought, before heading off to his own room. "Good night, big sister."

Chapter 7

BEN HAD BEEN SO TIRED THAT, DESPITE SOME strong and gusty overnight winds, he slept the whole night without waking up once. But when the morning came, his emotions were all tangled up. He was happy that Deke had a great home and was doing so well, but he was still confused about what "God's plan" was. And in the back of his mind, he was still puzzled about how Greg had known Dikran's shorter name.

But most of all, Ben was confused about what he believed. He had never felt like there was a God when all of the bad things were happening to him in the past. Before he was adopted, he had felt like he was alone. God never seemed to be there, and he had never felt like he was part of any plan.

Things were different, however, with little Deke. His past had been horrible, but listening to Grandpa tell the story, it *did* seem like a miracle that Deke was where he was now. A couple of times he had wondered if Grandpa was making the story up, but Grandpa would never do that. And there were all of those pictures. Deke's story *had* to be true.

As Ben headed down to breakfast, he hoped he would see Greg, and he hoped that the day would go by quickly. He needed to know the rest of Deke's story.

"Good morning, sleepyhead." Ben's mom smiled at him as she cleared her place. "Breakfast sure was good, or do you just want to wait for lunch?"

"Mom!" Ben looked around and saw that everyone else was done with breakfast. "I'm starved! I can't wait for lunch."

"Then grab a seat and dig in!" Grandma came walking out of the kitchen with a plate full of pancakes. The butter, syrup, and orange juice were already on the table.

"Grandma, how do you always know right when I am going to show up for breakfast?"

Grandma looked at Ben's mom, and they both smiled. "Ben, it's something that just comes with being a grandma. We just know. Just like a good grandpa knows exactly what kind of activity his grandson would love to do."

"Activity?" Ben's curiosity was aroused. "What activity does Grandpa have planned for today?"

Grandma looked at Ben with a smile on her face. "Let's just say it's something you have always wanted to do, and Grandpa now thinks you are old enough to handle the challenge."

"What challenge? What is it?" Ben searched his memory.

"While you are trying to figure it out, eat your breakfast." Ben's mom was pretending to be stern. "Your Grandpa won't start until you have a good meal."

Ben dug in, trying hard to figure out what he was going to be doing. He was almost done with his meal when Grandpa came walking into the kitchen. Ben saw that his hands were dirty, his work shirt had black smudges on it, and he was wiping his hands with a work rag.

A light went off in Ben's head. "The tractor? Do I get to drive the tractor?"

Grandpa just smiled down at Ben and nodded his head.

"Yippie!! I can't wait! When do I get to drive it? Can we go now?"

Grandpa looked at Ben's plate. "We are going to be gone for a while, so you first need to finish your breakfast."

"Gone?" Ben was trying to eat and talk at the same time. "Are we going somewhere?"

"Actually, Ben, this is sort of work related. You know the Peterson farm? The one about two miles down the road? Mr. Peterson's tractor broke down, and he really needs one right now. I am going to let him borrow mine for a week or two. With Raider, I can still pull things around if I need to."

Ben thought about that. "Am I going to get to drive the tractor all the way to the Peterson's farm? The whole two miles?"

Grandpa chuckled. "First things first. If you can drive it out of the barn, we will see about driving it down the road."

"I will, Grandpa!" Ben had finished his breakfast and jumped out of his chair to clear his place. "You wait and see! I can drive the tractor all the way to the Peterson's farm!"

Ben was good to his word. Not only was he able to drive the tractor out of the barn, he was able to back it up a bit, making the turn onto the road easier. Grandpa had given him a new straw hat to make him look more like a farmer, and Ben even found a wheat stalk to put in the corner of his mouth. He sat tall and proud in the driver's seat as he drove the tractor. Grandpa sat in the passenger seat but didn't have to take the wheel even once for the whole ride.

Mr. Peterson had been impressed when he saw Ben drive the tractor onto his farm and park it perfectly in front of his barn. The two men commented on how well Ben handled the tractor and then walked to the edge of Mr. Peterson's field to talk about farming things. Ben just sat in the driver's seat of the tractor, secretly wishing that Steven Keller could see him now.

Soon the two adults were done talking and strolled back to the tractor. Grandpa looked up at Ben and smiled. "Ben, Mr. Peterson would like to know if you could move the tractor to the edge of his field." Grandpa pointed to the field he was talking about. "I told him that I thought you could handle it. What do you think?"

Ben's face lit up. "You bet, Grandpa! Mr. Peterson, I can do it! Exactly where would you like me to park it?"

"You get that beast started, Ben, then just follow me to the spot. I'll walk ahead of you."

"Okay, Mr. Peterson, yes, sir!" Ben looked at Grandpa, expecting him to climb up into the passenger seat, but Grandpa just stepped back, smiled, and gestured for Ben to go ahead and drive. The smile on Ben's face spread from ear to ear. "Okay, Grandpa! Just watch."

Ten minutes later the tractor was parked right where Mr. Peterson wanted it, and the three farmers were headed inside for some cold lemonade. Ben loved the farmer's life and felt just like one of the men. The lemonade was as good as Grandma's.

As usual, Grandma's supper had been delicious. She had said that this one was *extra* special since it was the last one before Ben, his mom, and his sister returned home. Unlike all of the other suppers, Ben didn't want this one to end. He knew that storytime was going to happen, and he couldn't wait to hear the rest of Dikran's adventures, but he also didn't want tomorrow to come. He couldn't rush because he had to tell Grandma, his mom, and his sister every last detail about his tractor drive. They had insisted. He was a bit embarrassed over all the attention, but telling the story also made him feel special.

The cherry pie dessert was gone, and Ben saw the gleam in Grandpa's eye. He looked at his sister, and they nodded to each other, but before he could say a word, his mom spoke.

"Ben. Becca. Why don't you go ahead and clear your places? I think your grandpa is anxious to get started."

"Thanks, Mom!" They both leaped to their feet and cleared their places. Grandma got up and headed for the kitchen. "You two go upstairs and get ready. By the time you come back down, your cocoa will be waiting for you."

"Yay! Thanks, Grandma!" They both took off like rockets up the stairs to get ready. Just like Grandma had promised, their cocoa was ready by the time they came back down. Grandpa was also ready, standing there with the blankets and lantern. Ben looked at Grandpa's pockets, and it sure looked like there was something in there. He just smiled and took his mug of hot cocoa from Grandma.

As they headed down to the creek, Ben was a little concerned. "Grandpa?"

"Yes?"

"Greg wasn't here today. Is everything okay with him?"

Grandpa smiled and put his hand on Ben's shoulder. "Everything is fine. Greg is spending some extra time with his family. Just like you, they are leaving tomorrow, and he probably won't see them for a while. But he should be here before you leave. I think your mom doesn't plan on leaving until after lunch."

That seemed to satisfy Ben. "Okay. Thanks, Grandpa."

They arrived at the special story place and got all set up. As they snuggled into their places, Ben grinned and spoke before Grandpa could ask his standard opening question. "Yes, Grandpa, I remember where we left off. Mr. Dave had a Bible verse or story for all of Deke's tricks, and he was doing shows at schools. But how was that part of God's plan?"

Grandpa smiled at Ben's eagerness to get started. "It is *all* part of God's plan. There is something I would like to explain that can be hard to understand, but it helps to explain how God works." He winked at both of them. "Do you think you will be able to understand if I explain it carefully? It has everything to do with Mr. Dave and Dikran."

"Yes! Yes!" Ben and Rebecca were both eager to learn.

Grandpa leaned back in thought for a moment before explaining. "Look at the life of the apostle Paul. Remember, when he was still called Saul, what happened to him as he was on the road to…" Grandpa looked at both kids.

Rebecca knew the answer right away. "Damascus!"

"Right. And what was his life like before his encounter with the Lord?"

Rebecca again answered immediately. "He was a mean person. He acted very religious, but he was against anyone who loved Jesus."

"Right again. Why do you think God wanted to use Paul? Why use someone with a horrible past? Ben, we talked about this last night, remember?"

Ben was remembering what Grandpa had said about why Deke had such a hard start in life. "So people could see how much God could change someone's life?"

Grandpa clapped his hands together and smiled a big smile. "That is it exactly, Ben. Simply put, that is the Gospel message. So how do you think that applies to Dikran? What does his life tell you?"

Ben was beginning to understand. "So people who have had a bad start in life can see that there is… is always hope? Even when it doesn't seem that way?"

"That's right, Ben. And the Bible verses that Deke's tricks represent show a lot of ways that God takes care of us and how we are to live our lives. People usually remember things that they see a dog do, just like you remembered that verse from Matthew about being hungry and thirsty. And Deke has such a dramatic story that people remember what he does even better than usual. So Mr. Dave put some shows together using Deke to demonstrate how God loves us, can heal us, and can bless and use us. Dikran has become Mr. Dave's ministry."

Ben no longer had a bad look on his face when Grandpa was talking about things related to Jesus and God. Now he had an eager look, one that said he wanted to learn. "What exactly is a ministry?"

"It is something you do to help other people while teaching them about Jesus at the same time. Remember that Mr. Dave was doing a lot of shows with Deke? Now he also goes to churches and does his Bible shows for people there."

Grandpa smiled and dug into his pocket. "Here are a couple of pictures taken at a show Mr. Dave did with Deke at a church for the grade school kids." Grandpa first showed them a picture of Deke walking on his hind legs. "Mr. Dave connects this trick to the book of Proverbs and a verse that talks about walking uprightly. He calls this trick 'Walk like a man.'"

Ben and Rebecca stared at the picture, both thinking about the Bible verses that now went along with Deke's tricks. It gave the tricks more meaning knowing that there was a connection to the Bible in everything Deke did. As they both studied the picture, Grandpa held up the other picture. This one showed Deke lying on his performance table as Mr. Dave talked to the kids in the audience.

After shifting their gaze to the second picture, Rebecca spoke first. "Dikran looks so content just lying up there on the table. He seems to enjoy being in front of a crowd."

Grandpa nodded. "He does enjoy it. He is at ease performing anywhere Mr. Dave takes him. And Mr. Dave gave Deke's ministry a name. He calls it 'Guardian Dog Ministries.'"

Ben loved the name. "Guardian Dog Ministries. What a perfect name! Deke the Guardian Dog!"

Rebecca loved the name too. Then, after a moment, she turned to Grandpa. "What churches does Mr. Dave go to?"

Grandpa knew that this question was going to come up, and he couldn't hide the smile on his face. "I think he will go to any church that asks for him. He wants to reach as many people as he can, and whatever church God directs him to, he goes."

Ben and Rebecca looked at each other, their eyes wide. Rebecca grabbed her brother by the shoulders. "Maybe Dikran can come to our church! Maybe we can see him for real! Wouldn't that be so cool?"

Ben was once again out of his seat. "That would be awesome!" He looked at Grandpa. "That would be a miracle! A real live miracle!" Ben and Rebecca were so excited that neither one of them noticed the wide smile on Grandpa's face.

As their excitement quieted down, they resumed their seats, and Grandpa continued. "I agree, Ben. Deke's story is a real live miracle. But do you know what the *real* miracle in Deke's life is?"

"What, Grandpa?"

Grandpa leaned forward again and spoke as earnestly as he ever had. "Deke's life, from the very beginning and all the way until now, is a perfect example of the Christian life. Deke began his life as a poor, broken, starved, and abandoned puppy. Spiritually speaking, that is how all of us are at the beginning of our lives. Without Jesus, we are all like Deke was. Then, for Deke, God began to work in his life. He was rescued and he got a home. " Grandpa looked at Ben. "He was adopted into Mr. Dave and Mrs. Paula's home."

Ben looked from Grandpa to his sister. "You mean just like I was adopted into Mom and Becca's family?"

"Yes, Ben. Just like we can be adopted into God's family. Do you know how wonderful it is to have a family that you have been adopted into?"

Ben just nodded and blinked his eyes.

"And how lucky for you that you can be adopted twice!" Grandpa was looking at Ben with a gleam in his eye. "That makes you double special."

Ben didn't know what to say as he sat there, looking back and forth from Grandpa to Rebecca. He had tears in his eyes.

"And Deke was healed, just like we are spiritually healed when we are adopted into God's family. But did you know that if it ended there, it wouldn't be complete?"

Rebecca knew why. "Because nobody would know about it, right?"

"That's right. The Bible tells us that we are supposed to tell other people about Jesus. Sometimes the best way to tell people is to let them see what Jesus has done in our own lives."

Ben understood. "Just like Dikran going to churches and having Mr. Dave tell his story?"

"Yes, Ben. And then showing people what he can do now. Tricks and stunts that would have been impossible for a broken and starved little stray in Armenia. Impossible before God touched his life. So you see, Deke's whole life is a story of how God can heal people and give them a wonderful, new, and everlasting life. That is the true meaning behind the story of Dikran. That is why his story is so special."

When Grandpa had told Ben and Rebecca that it was time to head back to the house, neither one had complained. They just got up, gathered their blankets, and walked back to the house. Grandpa had walked between them with an arm draped over each of their shoulders. Maybe they didn't complain because Grandpa had told them that there was a surprise waiting for them at the house. Or maybe it was because Dikran's story felt so complete and satisfying to them.

As the whole family had gathered at the dining room table for an extra dessert of Grandma's freshly baked vanilla cake with chocolate frosting, Ben was the quietest of all. No longer did he have any questions about how the story would end. What was occupying his mind was that he now had a completely different way of looking at God. Dikran had taught him that. The story of Dikran hadn't gone the way he thought it would at all. He really hadn't known *how* it would go, but he never could have guessed that it would go the way it did.

But Grandpa had been right. This was the best story of all time. Dikran's story was wonderful, and as Ben lay in bed trying to stay awake, he now understood so clearly the connection he felt with the little runt from Armenia. And without even trying to, he found himself thanking God for Deke and for what Deke had taught him.

Even though Ben was tired, his mind was very active. As he stared at the ceiling, he wondered how he was going to get Deke to his church. He frowned as thoughts raced through his head. *My Sunday school teacher won't listen to me. She thinks I'm just a troublemaker.* Then he smiled as another thought came into his head. *But all the teachers love Becca. Maybe they will listen to her.*

With these conflicting thoughts swirling around in his head, Ben finally fell into a deep and uninterrupted sleep.

Chapter 8

MORNING CAME TO FIND BEN AS WELL RESTED as he had been for the whole week. As far as Dikran was concerned, he knew that everything was okay, which was probably why he had slept so well. But he still had things in his head that needed to be figured out. He wanted to talk with Greg, and he wanted to find out how to get Dikran to his church.

Before he had gone to bed, his mom had told him to strip his bed and pack all of his stuff before coming down for breakfast. They weren't leaving until after lunch, but Ben's mom didn't like everyone rushing around at the last minute trying to get ready.

Ben did as he had been told, then headed down the stairs. Halfway down, he heard the sound of the farm car leaving. He wondered who it was. As usual, he was the last one to eat. And, as usual, Grandma was ready with his plate.

She smiled and set down a plate of poached eggs, sausage, and hash browns. "You look like you slept well, Ben. Here is your breakfast. Dig in!"

"Thanks, Grandma! This smells great!" He looked around. "Where is everybody?"

"Well, let me see. Your grandfather and mom ran into town, and your sister is in the barn. I think she is spending some time with Raider."

Ben waited until he had finished his first mouthful. "Was that Grandpa and Mom leaving just now?"

"Yes, it was."

Ben didn't like the idea of Grandpa leaving. This was their last day, and he wanted to spend as much time with him as possible. "Where did they go? Do you know how long they will be gone?"

"I'm not sure." Grandma thought for a moment. "All they said was that they needed to get something. I don't know what. And your grandpa said that they would only be gone a couple of hours."

"Okay." *A couple of hours?* Ben didn't like that at all. After that, it would be lunchtime, and then it would be time to go. Ben looked up at Grandma. "Do you know if Greg will be here before we leave?"

Grandma smiled at Ben. "Greg got here an hour or so before you came down. He is in the west pasture looking at the stumps from those trees you cut down a couple of days ago. I think he is getting ready to pull them or grind them down."

"Oh, great!" Ben instantly began eating twice as fast.

Grandma laughed. "Ben, slow down! Greg isn't going anywhere."

"Okay, Grandma." Ben laughed at himself and slowed down. He tried to eat normally but still rush at the same time. As soon as he finished, he cleared his place, cleaned up, and asked Grandma if he could go out and talk to Greg.

"Of course, Ben. Just be careful if Greg is using any tools or equipment."

"I will, Grandma. Thanks."

Five minutes later Ben was headed out to the west pasture. He was wearing the straw hat that Grandpa had given him, and he had a wheat stalk in his mouth. A big part of him wanted to stay out here on the farm and never go back to the city. It took him a couple of minutes to walk out to where the tree stumps were.

"Hi, Greg!"

Greg looked up from his examination of the biggest stump. "Hey, farmer Benjamin! I heard you are quite the tractor driver!" He stuck his shovel in the ground and leaned on it, looking at Ben with an approving gleam in his eye. "Was it fun?"

Ben grinned and felt his face turn red. "It sure was! I love driving that tractor. I wish I could stay here and work on the farm every day like you do."

Greg took a rag out of his pocket and wiped his brow. He sighed deeply. "Well, there are times when I could use your help. You sure are a good worker."

Ben's face still felt red. "I love it here." Ben hesitated for a moment before going on. "Greg, you haven't been here very much this time. I missed you."

"I missed you too, Benjamin. My family was visiting, and I don't get to see them very often. They left for home this morning, and I probably won't see them again for a few years. That's why I was spending so much time with them."

"Oh." Ben thought about how hard it was for him to go one year without seeing Grandma and Grandpa. He was trying to figure out how to ask Greg about Deke when Greg brought the subject up for him.

"How did the story about Deke turn out?"

"It turned out great! It's the best story I have ever heard." Ben looked up. "How did you know that his

101

name is Deke? I know I told you his name was Dikran, and Grandpa said he hasn't talked to you about the story at all."

Greg laughed and wiped his brow again. "No, he hasn't said a word to me. But little Dikran's story is bigger than you think. Tell me, do you know where my family lives? Where I was born? Or the name I was given when I was born?"

Ben thought for a moment. "You mean your name isn't Greg?"

Greg smiled. "Oh, it is Greg. At least that's the way my name is said in English. The name I was born with is Grigor."

Ben looked puzzled. "Grigor? I've never heard of that name."

"You don't hear that name in America, but it is actually quite common where I was born. Do you have any idea where I am from?"

"No. I just know that it's far away. Where?"

Greg chuckled and patted Ben on the shoulder. "Actually, I think you do know where I am from. Or at least where it is." Greg looked intently at Ben, and then he smiled. "Ever hear of a city named Yerevan?"

Ben stood still for a couple of seconds as he searched his memory. "Yerevan?" Then his eyes got big. "Yerevan!" Ben's face lit up with excitement. "Armenia? That's where you were born? That's where Dikran was rescued! Did you know that?"

Greg smiled and put a big weathered hand on Ben's shoulder. "Yes, I know that. I am familiar with his story. One of my cousins lives in Los Angeles, and she knows some of the ladies who helped get Dikran to America."

Ben could hardly contain himself. "Wow! My Deke is so famous! Have you seen him in person?"

Greg shook his head. "No, I haven't, but my cousin was able to get some pictures of Deke from the ladies who got him to America. That's how your grandpa got all of those pictures. I gave them to him a few months ago."

Ben nodded to himself. Now he knew where Grandpa's pictures came from. "Too bad you haven't been able to see him for real."

Greg nodded his head. "But more and more people *are* seeing him. He has a very special ministry. Dikran is doing the Lord's work now."

"I know. I really wish I could see him." Ben hesitated for a moment. "Greg?"

"What is it, Benjamin?" Greg put a knee on the ground so he could look Ben in the eye.

Ben hesitated again.

Greg prodded him. "It's okay, just ask away."

Ben wasn't sure how to ask his question. "Do you…
I mean, all those things Grandpa said. About Deke
and Jesus and the Bible. Do *you* believe all that stuff?"

Greg looked off into the distance as though he
was thinking of faraway things. "You have heard his
story, Benjamin. Do you think all of those events just
happened by some coincidence? Abandoned dogs
in Armenia didn't stand much of a chance until just
recently. When Deke was a disfigured stray puppy in
the winter of 2012–2013, it would have taken a miracle for him to survive, and he did. And look at all
the events since then. His story is impossible, except
for God. And now He is using Deke to help spread
his simple Gospel message." Greg looked at Ben very
earnestly. "Can you see that, Benjamin?"

Ben nodded his head. "I didn't when Grandpa
began the story. But I think I understand now. I think.
You said it was a simple message?"

"It is. It is the simplest and most important message ever, and the Bible sums it up in one verse. It is
the most popular verse in the Bible. Do you know
what verse I am talking about? The Gospel of John
chapter 3, verse 16?"

"John 3:16." Ben repeated slowly. "That's how
Becca says it. She has said that verse to me a lot of
times, but I don't remember what it says."

*"For God so loved the world that He gave his one and
only Son, that whoever believes in him shall not perish but
have eternal life."* Greg smiled at Ben. "Everything that
Deke does and everything that he has been through
points to God's love and how He wants to save us.

You can't look at the story of Dikran without seeing the hand of God. It really is that simple."

Ben smiled and looked at Greg. "I believe that now. I really do. But why are there people like Steven Keller? People who are so mean and make fun of everyone? Even God?"

"Why did Dikran have so many bad things happen to him? Would you have been so drawn to his story if he hadn't overcome so many obstacles? Would you feel so connected to him if he had lived an easy, perfect life?"

Ben looked at the ground. "I love him because he had so much happen to him that wasn't good. He never let that bad stuff stop him."

"That's right." Greg stood up. "Look at Steven Keller the same way Dikran looked at the bad things that were in his way. You don't let the bad stuff make *you* bad. Dikran didn't. Steven Keller is just a test. Dealing with people like him can be quite a challenge, but you talk to God and read His Word, and He will give you the strength to face life's hardships the way Dikran has. That is what God wants you to do. And just like God is using Deke to show people what He can do, He wants to use you to show people the same thing, especially if they had a rough start in life like both you and Dikran had. In a big way, you are very much like Dikran." Greg smiled down at Ben, then turned his head and looked at the farmhouse. "I think your grandpa and mom have returned. Lunch, I believe, awaits!"

"Oh, wow!" Ben squinted and looked toward the sun, just like a farmer would. "I didn't realize how much time had passed. Are you going to have lunch with us?"

"Are you kidding?" Greg put his hand on Ben's shoulder and started walking to the house. "I wouldn't miss it for anything."

Lunch was over, and the car was almost loaded. Ben couldn't believe that they were already leaving. He had tears in his eyes as he put the last box in the trunk of the car. Everyone was there, and Ben felt a love for his family that was stronger than it had ever been. He was already planning in his head for next year's visit. He couldn't wait to return.

Grandpa was standing off to the side with his hands behind his back and an almost playful look on his face. He was looking back and forth between Ben and Rebecca. He caught Ben's eye and winked at him.

Ben cocked his head. "What is it, Grandpa?"

Rebecca looked at Grandpa too. "Why are your hands behind your back?"

Grandpa walked up to them. "You two didn't think we were going to send you home empty-handed, did you?" He brought his hands out from behind his back. Each hand held a gift-wrapped box about the size of a lunch pail. "One for you, my dear." He handed a box to Rebecca. "And one for our young farmer. These are from all of us."

Ben and Rebecca held their gifts with excitement. "Thanks, Grandpa and Grandma! Mom and Greg too!"

Ben had never been good at waiting to open gifts. "Can we open them now? Please?"

Grandpa had expected that. "Please do."

As excited as Ben was, he did remember his manners and let his sister go first. Rebecca looked around at everyone. She had a big smile on her face as she opened her gift.

"Oh, wow!" Her face lit right up. "A book about all of the best Bible stories! I love it!" She looked at her new book. "All about how the Bible stories have meaning for us today. I saw this book at our church bookstore and wanted it right away. Thank you so much!" She made her way around the group, hugging everyone. Holding her book tight, she turned and looked at Ben.

Ben smiled and felt a bit embarrassed with all the attention on him. His mom prodded him gently. "Go ahead, Ben. Open it up."

Despite all of the attention, Ben quickly opened his gift. Inside was a beautiful new Bible with a fancy black cover. Ben lifted the Bible out of the box and looked at it. He now had his own new Bible to go with his new beliefs. He smiled a big smile.

"Open it up, Ben." Grandpa came up to him and patted his head. Everyone else gathered around like they knew something that he didn't know. "Open it up and look at the first page."

Ben looked around at everyone, and then slowly opened his new Bible. He stood completely still for a moment, and his eyes got as big as saucers. Right there, before the beginning of Genesis on the page that is usually blank, was the best picture that he had ever seen. It was a picture of Dikran, and he was leaping right out of an open Bible. On the top of the page were the words "Guardian Dog" and right above Deke's head was the word "Dikran." Underneath his picture were two Bible verses.

Dikran

John 10:27–28

Ben had tears of joy in his eyes. His own personalized Bible, with Dikran right there on the front page to remind him of what God could do. "Thank you, everyone! Thank you so much!" He looked up. "What does John 10:27–28 say, Grandpa?"

Grandpa smiled at Ben. "Wait until you are on the road, then read it and think about the meaning. It is just about the best of all of God's promises. I will only say that you will probably find a connection to your favorite dog in that promise."

Ben was as content and happy as he had ever been in his life. He was sad that they were leaving the farm, but his happiness at the way his life was going was way bigger than the sad part. He had everyone's email addresses so he could talk to them on his computer at home, and he had a whole new batch of great memories that he would keep for his entire life.

Goodbyes were said, and they climbed into the car. Ben and Rebecca both had tears in their eyes as the car pulled onto the road heading south, and they watched and waved until they could no longer see their grandparents or Greg. Even then, they stared back toward the farm for several more minutes, not wanting to let go of the most wonderful vacation they had ever had.

Epilogue

BEN WAS IN HIS PAJAMAS, SITTING ON THE edge of his bed. He was tired from the long ride home but not ready to sleep. Too many things were going through his mind. He was thinking about the trip back home and how he had done just what Grandpa had told him to do. Once they were on the main highway heading home, he had opened his new Bible and found — with Rebecca's help — John 10:27–28 and read the verses, over and over. He had then turned to the front of his Bible and looked at the picture of Dikran leaping from the Bible. He *did* see the connection, just as Grandpa had said he would. He had then turned back to the two verses in John's Gospel and read them again. He had practically memorized them before getting halfway home, and he would close his eyes and practice saying them in his head.

> *My sheep listen to my voice; I know them, and they follow me. I give them eternal life, and they shall never perish; no one can snatch them out of my hand.*

Ben's mind came back to the present. He smiled as he now understood what it meant to be a sheep, and how he needed a shepherd. A guardian. Jesus was his Guardian, just like Dikran was a guardian. The best guardian dog ever. Dikran would never let a wolf snatch one of his sheep away, and Jesus would never let anyone snatch one of His sheep away, either. Ben smiled. "Not even Steven Keller can snatch me away!"

Rebecca's voice came from down the hall. "Did you say something, Ben?"

"No." Ben stood up and pulled his covers back. "Just talking to myself. Goodnight, Becca."

"Goodnight, Ben. We sure had a fun vacation, didn't we?"

"We sure did." Ben looked up as his mom walked into the room. She sat on the edge of his bed and finished tucking him in. She then smiled down at him. "I'm glad you had such a fun time."

"I sure did, Mom. It was great. I just wish…"

"Wish what?" His mom leaned down and kissed him on the forehead. "What are you wishing for?"

"I wish I could see Dikran. I wish he would come to our church."

"I know." Ben's mom got up and headed for the door. "Have a good night's sleep, Ben." She switched off the bedroom light and turned back to Ben. "Oh, I forgot to tell you. When I was in town with your grandpa this morning, I made a couple of phone calls."

Ben leaned up on his elbow. "Who did you call?"

"The first call was to our church. I talked to Pastor Brian. I had a few questions for him."

Ben wondered what her questions were. "Who was the second call to?"

"Um." Ben's mom looked like she was pretending to remember something. "Some place called Guardian

Dog Ministries." She smiled and turned to walk out of the room. "I talked to a man named Mr. Dave."

Ben's eyes just about popped out of his head.

The End

About the Author
David M. Guild

DAVE LIVES IN GLENDORA, CALIFORNIA, WITH his wife, Paula, and their three adopted dogs — Greta, Jackie, and Dikran. Their son, John, is serving in the United States Navy.

Dave has been professionally training dogs since 1980, having trained dogs for law enforcement, the entertainment industry, and for dog owners all over Southern California. He is actively involved in rehabilitating rescued dogs that have been adopted into new homes.

Dave and his family have attended a Calvary Chapel church near their home since 1999 and share Dikran's story through Guardian Dog Ministries with churches and schools wherever God leads.

Armenian Gampr sources

THE FOLLOWING TWO WEBSITES ARE WHERE I got most of my information on Armenian Gamprs.

1. Armenian Gampr Club of America at <gampr.org>
2. Armenian Gampr breed information at <dogbreedinfo.com/a/armeniangampr>

Image Citations

Image Number and Credit

1. Cover photo of Dikran   John A. Guild

Prologue
2. Sketch Ben &   David M. Guild / Paul Berry
   Rebecca walking home

Chapter 1
3. Sketch greeting   David M. Guild/Paul Berry
   Grandma & Grandpa

Chapter 2
4. Sketch ready for story   David M. Guild / Paul Berry
5. Photo Gampr guarding sheep   website breedinfo.ru

Chapter 3
6. Photo Puppy Gampr   website doglib.com
7. Photo City of Yerevan   website kudoybook.com
8. Photo Dikran side view   Ovsanna Hovsepyan
   in Armenia
9. Photo Dikran lying   Ovsanna Hovsepyan
   down in Armenia

Chapter 4
10. Sketch kids greeting GregDavid M. Guild / Paul Berry
11. Photo Dikran on surgery table   Ovsanna Hovsepyan
12. Photo Dikran walking   Ovsanna Hovsepyan
    bandaged legs
13. Photo Ovsanna holding Dikran   Ovsanna Hovsepyan

14. Photo Dikran in crate — Ovsanna Hovsepyan
15. Photo Dikran's Aunties — Laura Manukian
16. Photo Laura holding Dikran — Laura Manukian

Chapter 5
17. Photo Dikran in my lap — Paula Guild
18. Photo Dikran asleep in dog run — David M. Guild
19. Photo Dikran's legs healing — David M. Guild
20. Photo Dikran's legs healed — David M. Guild
21. Photo the three dogs — David M. Guild

Chapter 6
22. Photo Dikran jumping through hoop — Paula Guild
23. PhotoDikran sitting upright on table — Paula Guild
24. Photo Dikran walking on hind legs — Paula Guild
25. Photo Dikran jumping through hoop — John A. Guild
26. Photo Dikran sitting upright on table — Paula Guild

Chapter 7
27. Photo Dikran walking on hind legs — Rob Wiltsey
28. Photo Dikran lying on table — Rob Wiltsey
29. Sketch Ben, Rebecca, Grandpa — David M. Guild / Paul Berry

Chapter 8
30. Sketch Ben & Greg — David M. Guild / Paul Berry
31. Photo Dikran jumping from Bible — Paula Guild / Mark Thiel

Back Cover
4. Sketch ready for Story — David M. Guild / Paul Berry

About the Author
32. Dikran and myself on mountain — John A. Guild

CPSIA information can be obtained
at www.ICGtesting.com
Printed in the USA
FSOW03n0447151217
41937FS

9 781545 618523